5-minute microwave canning

Includes
fruits, preserves, chutneys, sauces and much more!

Isabel Webb

The Five Mile Press

The Five Mile Press Pty Ltd
415 Jackson St, San Francisco
CA 94111 USA
www.fivemile.com.au

Copyright © Isabel Webb, 2009
All rights reserved

First published 2009
This edition published 2010

Printed in China (August 2010)

Cover design by Brad Maxwell
Page design by Zoë Murphy
Cover photograph: Photolibrary

ISBN: 978 1 74248 477 8

Contents

Preface

When my first book on canning fruit in the microwave oven *Microwave Bottling: Fruits, Jams, Jellies, Pickles & Sauces* was published in 1989 it caused a sensation. I wrote it after literally hundreds of hours experimenting and developing recipes in my own kitchen. I was the first person to advocate this ultra-simple canning method. And the book was an instant success, reprinting many times.

From this idea, my next concept in microwave canning emerged: the "Just Fruit" method. As the name suggests, you don't need to put anything in the jar except the fruit itself. No sugar or liquid is added, making this method perfect for the weight-conscious as well as those on special diets. And what could be easier? I published this new concept in my next book *More Microwave Bottling*.

Twenty years on, I still receive letters and phone calls asking where to buy my books on microwave canning and preserving, so felt it was high time to write this revised, expanded edition which combines all my best recipes.

One of the beauties of this method is that you use recycled food jars with metal lids. "But you can't put metal in the microwave," is the invariable response when people hear this. Where did the conviction that you can't put any metal in the microwave come from? When microwave ovens first came on the market several people used their expensive gold- or silver-rimmed dinner plates to heat food in their microwave ovens.

The gold or silver edging consisted of a metallic paint made up of tiny specks of metal, which caused the microwaves to jump about, causing arcing and damaging the plates.

After receiving several complaints the manufacturers declared that no metal was to be put in the microwave. But as leading microwave manufacturers now freely acknowledge, you can safely put a certain ratio of metal in the microwave. In fact, many microwave ovens come equipped with metal plate-stackers.

So I can assure you that it's quite safe to put metal objects in your microwave oven as long as you don't exceed the ratio of 30 percent metal to 70 percent of other substances, and you leave a space of one inch between each jar, and also between the jars and the sides of the oven.

When canning and preserving in a microwave oven the finished products are closer to their natural form than with more conventional methods. They also boast enhanced color, shape, flavor, and keeping quality, as well as retaining their nutritional value.

Even after decades of using my microwave to bottle fruit I am still astonished at the excellent results.

For me, microwave canning has revolutionized the preserving of fruit as well as the making of preserves, jellies, chutneys, pickles, sauces, glacé fruit, and fruit liqueurs. If you carefully follow the recipes in this book you will rediscover the immense pleasure to be gained from canning your own fruit and making your own preserves. And you won't believe how easy it is until you try it for yourself.

I've called this new book *5-Minute Microwave Canning* but in fact most fruits take even less than five minutes. It all depends on the amount of fruit and the size of the bottle. As you'll see, it's very quick and easy!

I hope this book introduces a new generation to the joys of microwave canning and preserving as well as providing recipes for the many people who have requested them.

Isabel Webb, 2009

1

Before You Begin

It's essential to read this chapter carefully before you turn to *any* of the chapters in this book. To accommodate the wattage of all microwave ovens I have given instructions for microwaves from 650 watts through to 1500 watts. Remember, the higher the wattage the faster the food cooks. Speed of cooking is not always a good thing, especially in fruit canning. If cooked too fast the liquid will reach boiling point, causing spillage, before the fruit has time to cook through.

As I've mentioned in my Preface it's perfectly safe to use metal in the microwave, as long as the ratio of metal to other materials is correct. I've been putting metal lids in the microwave oven for more than twenty years – with great success.

Sealed Jars in Your Microwave

A processed bottle of fruit doesn't vacuum seal until about 5–10 minutes after leaving the microwave oven, as cooling takes place. Because the metal lid has a higher coefficient of expansion than glass the expanding air and liquid has space to escape between lid and jar during the cooking time, thus there is no fear of the jar breaking.

Metal and Your Microwave

Microwaves will not penetrate metal. Therefore, if a ratio of no more than 30 percent metal to 70 percent of other substances is used, the

cooking times are not affected. This ratio is accepted by leading manufacturers as safe to both food and to the microwave oven. The amount of metal in the lids of food jars is far below the specified ratio, and no cooking interruption takes place.

Nowadays, many microwave food manufacturers package their product in foil containers for take-away meals, and microwave ovens come equipped with metal plate-stackers. This speaks for itself.

I suggest that you process only up to four bottles at the one time. But this is not because the quantity of metal would increase (it would still be well below the acceptable ratio) but because the cooking times would no longer be accurate.

As a precaution, always allow a space of at least 1¼ inches between each jar and also between the jars and the oven wall.

Arcing

Microwaves travel in straight lines. If they hit a metal object they bounce off. If there is another metal object directly in their path and at no more than 1¼ inches away they will bounce onto it, setting up a circuit, thus arcing. However, because the lids on the jars are round the micro-waves are prevented from bouncing back in a straight line, thus no arcing occurs.

Two "Musts"

- Make sure the jars to be used fit in your microwave oven with their lids on.
- Make sure there's no excess water on the microwave carousel as any moisture could affect the cooking times.

Power Variations

Remember that every microwave oven, like any other type of oven, will cook slightly differently. However, with microwaves there are three main reasons the power input may alter:

1. Several home appliances are being used at the same time.
2. You're at the end of a power line (both in the country and in city areas).
3. Heavy electrical machinery is being used nearby.

Check the Wattage

The most important thing to know is the power of the microwave oven you are using. Cooking times in this book are for a 650-watt microwave. If your oven has less or more power, use the chart below to vary the power setting and cook for the suggested times in each recipe. If you don't know the power of your microwave oven the place to look is either on the inside or back of the oven. A plaque will show the output power.

MICROWAVE POWER	POWER SETTING
500–600 watts	HIGH (100% microwaves)
650–750 watts	MEDIUM HIGH (75% microwaves)
800–1000 watts	MEDIUM (50% microwaves)
1000–1500 watts	MEDIUM LOW (35% microwaves)

Equipment

The microwave method eliminates the need for elaborate equipment. You will need:

- a large microwave-proof bowl with a cover
- a spoon, preferably wooden
- recycled food jars.

Using Recycled Jars

Recycled food jars are ideal for microwave canning provided:

- Their lids are the metal screw-on variety, in good condition. Metal lids are treated on the inside with a special food lacquer to protect them from corrosive food acids. It is important to check that this film is not damaged in any way and that the lids are in "as new" condition and fit perfectly.
- The lids are fitted with a built-in rubber sealing ring.
- The jars are not chipped or cracked. Their rims must be smooth and free from any chips, ridges, or any imperfections. Damaged jars won't seal properly and the fruit will spoil.

NOTE: Plastic lids must not be used.

Sterilizing Your Equipment

1. Clean jars thoroughly in hot water, removing any adhesions with a bottle brush before sterilizing.
2. Half-fill jars with cold water and cook on HIGH until water boils (about 2 minutes per jar).
3. Remove jars from microwave and fill the lids of the jars with the hot water.
4. Pour away water before fruit is packed into jars. If the jars used are washed, clean and free from any foreign particles it isn't necessary to sterilize them before filling with fruit because when the bottles of fruit are cooking all is sterilized at the same time.

2

Fruit Canning in the Microwave

With this quick and easy microwave method forget the hours or even days involved in the traditional canning method. Just think in minutes. And the results are fabulous, and hard to beat for flavor, texture and – most importantly – nutritional value. If you've never tried canning in the microwave, now's the time to start. I'm sure you'll wonder what took you so long to try it! Following are some tips to help make your canning a complete success.

Preparing and Packing the Fruit
1. Never use fruit straight from the refrigerator. Always use it at room temperature. Cold fruit will alter cooking times.
2. Choose unblemished fruit. Wash well in cold water.
3. Peel, core, slice, or dice fruit according to the recipe. Check the recipe for any precooking, soaking or other preparation necessary.
4. Pack fruit into clean, sterilized jars. If filling jars to capacity, leave at least half an inch below the lip of the jar. Gently tap the bottom of each jar on the palm of your hand to ensure firm packing. But don't worry if jars are not filled to capacity, as air will be expelled during cooking. (The metal lid will expand on heating, allowing excess air to escape.)
5. Screw lids on fully before cooking. Don't remove lids when bottles are still hot.

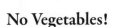

No Vegetables!
NEVER attempt to preserve vegetables in your microwave. Government health authorities warn that this could be fatal because vegetables do *not* contain the acid content (found in fruit) which inhibits the growth of botulism.

Brine
Brine is sometimes used with preserved tomatoes to enhance their flavor and appearance. To make brine, dissolve ¼ cup of cooking salt in 10 cups of water.

Citric Acid
Some fruits (for example, cantaloupe, and mangoes) are low in natural fruit acids and will not preserve successfully unless citric acid is added. Check individual recipes for amounts required.

Syrup
Syrup can be used with all fruit canning if desired. The strength of the syrup used can be adjusted according to taste, but some fruits require heavier syrups than others for best results. The recipes in this chapter specify light, medium or heavy syrup.

TYPE OF SYRUP	SUGAR REQUIRED
Light Syrup	one part sugar to three parts water e.g. 1 cup sugar to 3 cups water
Medium Syrup	one part sugar to two parts water e.g. 1 cup sugar to 2 cups water
Heavy Syrup	one part sugar to one part water e.g. 1 cup sugar to 1 cup water

Making the Syrup

Place the sugar and water in a microwave-proof bowl or jug and cook in a microwave oven on HIGH. Boil for about 2 minutes, or until the sugar has completely dissolved. Stir once during this time. For those wishing to avoid sugar, please note that it's possible to bottle fruit in the microwave without adding syrup. See *"Just Fruit" Canning* on page 54.

Jar Capacity

JAR SIZE	FRUIT WEIGHT	LIQUID NEEDED
8 ounces	3 ounces	½–1 cup
13 ounces	5 ounces	¾–1 cup
19 ounces	10 ounces	1–1½ cups
27 ounces	16 ounces	1½–2 cups
29 ounces	16 ounces	2–2¼ cups

Adding the Syrup to the Fruit

The syrup should be lukewarm when added to the jars packed with fruit. If it has cooled, cook for an additional 1–2 minutes.

Alternative Sweeteners for Making Syrup

SWEETENER	SUGGESTED AMOUNTS
honey or light molasses	3–4 tablespoons to 1 cup of water
glucose	4 ounces to 1 cup of water
artificial sweeteners	1 tablet for 1 cup of water

Note: Artificial sweeteners can cause a bitter flavor after storing. To avoid this, preserve the fruit in water and add the sweetener on serving.

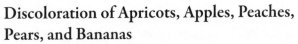

Discoloration of Apricots, Apples, Peaches, Pears, and Bananas

To help prevent the discoloration of these fruits during storage, soak prepared fruit in a solution of 2 cups water to the juice of 1 lemon (or ½ teaspoon sodium metabisulfite to one cup of water) for a few minutes before rinsing and canning.

Cooking the Fruit

Each recipe contains a table showing oven settings and cooking times required to bring the inside of the fruit to 180°F, thus eliminating all microbes and ensuring a good seal. The times given are those needed for firm, ripe fruit at room temperature. Less cooking time is needed for soft fruits such as grapes and berries than for hard fruits such as apples and pears, as you will see from individual recipes.

Arrange no more than four jars in a circle on the carousel, leaving at least one inch between each jar and the same distance between the jars and the oven wall.

Cooling the Fruit and Checking the Seal

1. After cooking, remove jars from the microwave oven and stand on a rack, a board or several sheets of newspaper to cool. Don't touch lids as some hot liquid or steam could escape and burn.
2. Allow jars to cool for several hours or overnight before checking seals. Recycled jars with a screw-type lid will be concave when sealed.
3. Stand cold jars upside-down for at least one hour and check for any leakage. If leakage occurs, the jars have not sealed.
4. If jars have not sealed, immediately check that the correct lid is being used and that there are no food particles on the rim of the jar. Re-process in microwave for same time as previously. Then repeat

Steps 1–4. If fruit is not reprocessed, it must be refrigerated and eaten with two to three days.

5. If there is no leakage and the lids remain firm, a good vacuum has been achieved and the fruit will keep well.

Storing the Fruit

- Label and date jars.
- Store in a cool, dark place.
- For optimum color, flavor, and nutritional value all preserved fruit is best used within 12 months of being made.
- Once opened, jars of preserved fruit must be stored in the refrigerator and eaten within two to three days.

Shelf Life

It isn't wise to keep bottled fruit for years, although I have used fruit after two years and found it to be perfect. However, for optimum color and flavor and nutritional value I suggest you use your bottled fruit within 12 months. Then they can be replaced by new season's fruit.

DOs and DON'Ts

The following is a checklist of the main DOs and DON'Ts of microwave fruit canning:

- Make sure fruit is of good, sound quality and is at room temperature.
- Clean fruit well in cold water before placing in sterilized jars. Soak apricots, apples, peaches, and pears as described on page 14 to prevent discoloration.
- It's all right if jars are not quite dry, as a little moisture helps the fruit slide into position.
- DON'T use rusty, damaged, or pitted lids.

- DON'T use jars that have the push down spring clip to fasten the lid. They are storing jars not preserving jars. Sometimes if the clip is very hard to close the pressure in the jar during cooking isn't great enough to lift the lid and allow the hot air and juices to come away freely.
- Always use the conventional or the recycled screw type food jars only. (Read more about using recycled food jars on page 54.)
- Make sure lids and clips are firmly secured.
- Check that your oven is on the correct setting.
- After cooking, stand jars on a cake rack, chopping board or several layers of newspaper. This prevents damage to jars and surfaces.
- DON'T remove clips or lids while bottles are still hot. Allow to cool overnight or for several hours.
- Check the seal (see page 14). If no liquid oozes out you have achieved a good result. If liquid escapes, fruit may have been caught under the lid or the wrong lid may have been used. Rectify the problem before reprocessing in the oven. Alternatively, the fruit must be treated as any other jar of fruit just opened, and eaten within a couple of days.
- Store in a cool, dark place to ensure good color and nutritional value for an optimum period.
- DON'T try to reseal a half-used jar. Once a jar has been opened, the contents must be kept refrigerated and used within a few days.

Troubleshooting

Below are some common microwave canning problems, and the most likely reason for them:

PROBLEM	MOST LIKELY REASON
Fruit of poor color	– Overripe fruit used.

	– Jar processed for too long.
	– Storage area either too light or too warm.
Jar didn't seal	– The microwave setting was too low (see page 14).
	– Bruised, damaged or overripe fruit used.
	– Bottled fruit not cooked long enough, so perfect seal not achieved.
	– Jar not stored in cool, dark place.
	– Mold and fermentation have affected the seal.
	– Bacteria formed. This sometimes occurs in low-acid fruits. Check the recipe for the correct quantity of citric acid to be added.
	– An unclean, unsterilized jar was used.
Apricots, apples, peaches or pears discolored during storage	– Fruit acids have caused browning. Follow directions on page 14.

Cooking Times

The cooking times in this chapter are for one jar in a 650-watt microwave oven. If you wish to preserve more than one jar at a time, note the following:

- For microwave oven capacity of 500 up to 1500 watts add 1 minute extra cooking time for each additional jar using the appropriate oven setting for your oven. See page 9.

- When using different sized jars at the same time always take the stated cooking time of the largest jar first, then add 1 or 2 minutes cooking time for every extra jar, as each recipe suggests.
- Remember that if you have only one cup of fruit in a 2 cup plus size jar, you must calculate your cooking time by the amount of fruit, not by the jar size.
- A processed bottle of fruit seals about 5 minutes after leaving the microwave oven, as cooling takes place.
- Metal lids must be used, as metal has a higher coefficient of expansion than glass, and any expanding air and liquid has space to escape between lid and jar.
- Don't use more than four jars at any one time, as cooking times will vary.

Cup Measurements

In the following recipes the amount of fruit is sometimes given in cupfuls. Please note that these are approximate measures only, as fruit size varies.

Apples

INGREDIENTS
cooking apples
water
Medium Syrup (see page 12)

METHOD
1. Peel and core apples, then dice, slice into circles, or quarter. Immerse fruit in suggested solution (see page 14) to prevent discoloring.
2. When ready to use, drain and rinse fruit in fresh cold water.
3. Pack fruit into clean, sterilized jars.
4. Fill jars to overflowing with Medium Syrup. Fit lids on jars.
5. Cook according to table below.

JAR SIZE	OVEN SETTING	COOKING TIME
8 ounces	medium high	5 minutes
16 ounces	medium high	8 minutes
28 ounces	medium high	12 minutes

Note: Cooking times are for 1 jar. Add 2 minutes for every additional jar.

6. Cool and store according to directions on pages 14–15.

Check the power of your microwave and adjust the setting if necessary (see page 9).

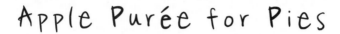

Apple Purée for Pies

INGREDIENTS

6 – 8 cooking apples

½ cup water

8 ozs sugar

METHOD

1. Wash apples and chop roughly. There is no need to peel or core them.
2. Place chopped fruit and water in a microwave-proof bowl and cover. Cook on HIGH until soft and pulpy (about 10 minutes).
3. Remove from oven and allow to stand, covered, for 5 minutes.
4. Press mixture through a sieve or Mouli, or purée in a food-processor. Stir in sugar.
5. Fill clean, sterilized jars with apple pulp. Fit lids on jars.
6. Cook according to table below.

JAR SIZE	OVEN SETTING	COOKING TIME
8 ounces	medium high	3 minutes
16 ounces	medium high	3 minutes
28 ounces	medium high	4 minutes

Note: Cooking times are for 1 jar. Add 2 minutes for every additional jar.

7. Cool and store according to directions on pages 14–15.

Check the power of your microwave and adjust the setting if necessary (see page 9).

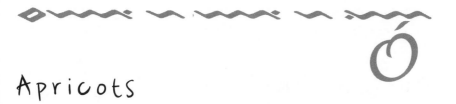

Apricots

INGREDIENTS

apricots

Medium Syrup (see page 12)

METHOD

1. Choose firm, ripe unblemished apricots and wash. They can be halved or, if small, left whole. To halve, cut around the natural line with a stainless steel knife and twist apart. Remove and discard stones. Immerse fruit in suggested solution to prevent discoloration (see page 14).
2. Pack fruit into clean, sterilized jars.
3. Fill jars to overflowing with Medium Syrup. Fit lids on jars.
4. Cook according to table below.

JAR SIZE	OVEN SETTING	COOKING TIME
8 ounces	medium high	5 minutes
16 ounces	medium high	8 minutes
28 ounces	medium high	12 minutes

Note: Cooking times are for 1 jar. Add 2 minutes for every additional jar.

5. Cool and store according to directions on pages 14–15.

Check the power of your microwave and adjust the setting if necessary (see page 9).

Apricot Purée for Pies

INGREDIENTS

2 lbs apricots

1 cup water

1 cup sugar

METHOD

1. Wash apricots and halve by cutting around the natural line with a stainless steel knife. Twist halves apart. Remove and discard stones.
2. Place fruit and water in a microwave-proof bowl and cover. Cook on HIGH until soft and pulpy (about 7 minutes).
3. Remove from oven and allow to stand, covered, for 5 minutes.
4. Press mixture through a sieve or Mouli, or purée in a food-processor. Stir in sugar.
5. Fill clean, sterilized jars with apricot pulp. Fit lids on jars.
6. Cook according to the table below.

JAR SIZE	OVEN SETTING	COOKING TIME
8 ounces	medium high	3 minutes
16 ounces	medium high	3 minutes
28 ounces	medium high	4 minutes

Note: Cooking times are for 1 jar. Add 2 minutes for every additional jar.

7. Cool and store according to directions on pages 14–15.

Check the power of your microwave and adjust the setting if necessary (see page 9).

Spicy Apricots and Almonds

INGREDIENTS

apricots

almonds, at least 2 for each apricot

Mixed spice, ½ teaspoon for every 1 cup of syrup

Medium Syrup (see page 12)

METHOD

1. Blanch almonds by placing them in a microwave-proof bowl, covering them with water and heating on HIGH for 2–3 minutes. Cool, then squeeze almonds between fingers to remove brown skins.
2. Pack prepared apricots into clean, sterilized jars, placing almonds between each piece of fruit.
3. Add mixed spice to syrup.
4. Fill jars to overflowing with syrup mixture. Fit lids on jars.
5. Cook according to table below.

JAR SIZE	OVEN SETTING	COOKING TIME
8 ounces	medium high	5 minutes
16 ounces	medium high	8 minutes
28 ounces	medium high	12 minutes

Note: Cooking times are for 1 jar. Add 2 minutes for every additional jar.

6. Cool and store according to directions on pages 14–15.

Check the power of your microwave and adjust the setting if necessary (see page 9).

Bananas

INGREDIENTS

bananas

1 teaspoon citric acid for every 3 cups of syrup

Medium Syrup (see page 12)

METHOD

1. Choose firm, ripe bananas with no bruises or blemishes. Peel under cold water to prevent discoloring. Pat dry when ready to use, or soak in suggested solutions (see page 14).
2. Cut into thick slices or lengths to fit selected jars.
3. Pack fruit into clean, sterilized jars.
4. Dissolve citric acid in Medium Syrup.
5. Fill jars to overflowing with syrup mixture.
6. Cook according to table below.

JAR SIZE	OVEN SETTING	COOKING TIME
8 ounces	medium high	3 minutes
16 ounces	medium high	4 minutes
28 ounces	medium high	5 minutes

Note: Cooking times are for 1 jar. Add 2 minutes for every additional jar.

7. Cool and store according to directions on pages 14–15.

Check the power of your microwave and adjust the setting if necessary (see page 9).

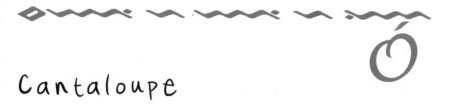

Cantaloupe

INGREDIENTS

cantaloupe

3 teaspoons citric acid for every 4 cups of syrup

Medium Syrup (see page 12)

METHOD

1. Choose full, ripe cantaloupe. Peel and seed. Round out small balls with a melon-baller, slice or dice.
2. Pack fruit into clean, sterilized jars.
3. Dissolve citric acid in Medium Syrup.
4. Fill jars to overflowing with syrup mixture. Fit lids on jars.
5. Cook according to table below.

JAR SIZE	OVEN SETTING	COOKING TIME
8 ounces	medium high	4 minutes
16 ounces	medium high	5 minutes
28 ounces	medium high	6 minutes

Note: Cooking times are for 1 jar. Add 2 minutes for every additional jar.

6. Cool and store according to directions on page 14.

Check the power of your microwave and adjust the setting if necessary (see page 9).

Carambola (Star Fruit)

INGREDIENTS

carambola (star fruit)

Light Syrup (see page 12)

2 teaspoons lemon juice to every cup of syrup

METHOD

1. Wash, cut half inch thick slices crosswise, and remove seeds.
2. Fill clean sterilized jars with star fruit, cover with syrup. Fit lids on jars.
3. Cook according to table below.

JAR SIZE	OVEN SETTING	COOKING TIME
8 ounces	medium high	3 minutes
16 ounces	medium high	5 minutes
28 ounces	medium high	7 minutes

Note: Cooking times are for 1 jar. Add 2 minutes for every additional jar.

4. Cool and store according to directions on pages 14–15.

Check the power of your microwave and adjust the setting if necessary (see page 9).

Cherries

INGREDIENTS

cherries

Medium Syrup (see page 12)

METHOD

1. Discard any damaged or blemished cherries and wash the rest clean. If desired, remove stones with a cherry-stoner.
2. Pack fruit into clean, sterilized jars.
3. Fill jars to overflowing with Medium Syrup. Fit lids on jars.
4. Cook according to table below.

JAR SIZE	OVEN SETTING	COOKING TIME
8 ounces	medium high	5 minutes
16 ounces	medium high	8 minutes
28 ounces	medium high	12 minutes

Note: Cooking times are for 1 jar. Add 2 minutes for every additional jar.

5. Cool and store according to directions on pages 14–15.

Check the power of your microwave and adjust the setting if necessary (see page 9).

Cherries and Kirsch

INGREDIENTS

2 lbs dark red or bing cherries

1 cup sweet red wine

2 tablespoons Kirsch

2 tablespoons sugar

1 teaspoon ground cinnamon

4–5 whole cloves

METHOD

1. Discard any damaged or blemished cherries and wash the remainder clean. If desired, remove stones with a cherry-stoner.
2. Place all other ingredients into a microwave-proof bowl, bring to boiling point on HIGH for about 2–3 minutes. Stir to dissolve sugar. Remove cloves.
3. Pack fruit into clean, sterilized jars. Fill with syrup. Fit lids on jars.
4. Cook according to table below.

JAR SIZE	OVEN SETTING	COOKING TIME
8 ounces	medium high	5 minutes
16 ounces	medium high	8 minutes
28 ounces	medium high	12 minutes

Note: Cooking times are for 1 jar. Add 2 minutes for every additional jar.

5. Cool and store according to directions on pages 14–15.

Check the power of your microwave and adjust the setting if necessary (see page 9).

Feijoa

INGREDIENTS
24 feijoa (approx.)
3–4 cups Medium Syrup (see page 12)
2 teaspoons lemon juice to every cup of syrup

METHOD
1. Peel and thickly slice feijoa or split lengthwise.
2. Pack feijoa into clean, sterilized jars, cover with syrup. Fit lids on jars.
3. Cook according to table below.

JAR SIZE	OVEN SETTING	COOKING TIME
8 ounces	medium high	3 minutes
16 ounces	medium high	5 minutes
28 ounces	medium high	7 minutes

Note: Cooking times are for 1 jar. Add 1 minute for every additional jar.

4. Cool and store according to directions on pages 14–15.

Check the power of your microwave and adjust the setting if necessary (see page 9).

Feijoa Fruit Salad

INGREDIENTS

6 feijoa

2 cups strawberries

1 banana

3 oranges, divided into segments

3 apples, diced

2 tablespoons lemon juice

sugar to taste

METHOD

1. Peel feijoa, banana, oranges, and apples, cut into slices or dice.
    Cut strawberries in half.
2. Place into bowl, add lemon juice and sugar to taste, mix together.
3. Fill clean, sterilized jars with fruit salad. Fit lids on jars.
4. Cook according to table below.

JAR SIZE	OVEN SETTING	COOKING TIME
8 ounces	medium high	3 minutes
16 ounces	medium high	4 minutes
28 ounces	medium high	5 minutes

Note: Cooking times are for 1 jar. Add 1 minute for every additional jar.

5. Cool and store according to directions on pages 14–15.

Check the power of your microwave and adjust the setting if necessary (see page 9).

Fruit Salad

INGREDIENTS

mixture of fruits high in citric acid (apples, apricots, cherries, grapes, pineapples, peaches, and oranges)

Medium Syrup (see page 12)

METHOD

1. Choose ripe fruits high in citric acid. Fresh fruits low in citric acid (such as bananas, cantaloupes, pawpaws, figs, and mangoes) can be added when preserved fruit salad is served.
2. Peel fruit, if necessary, and cut or dice. Mix together.
3. Pack fruit into clean, sterilized jars.
4. Fill jars to overflowing with Medium Syrup. Fit lids on jars.
5. Cook according to table below.

JAR SIZE	OVEN SETTING	COOKING TIME
8 ounces	medium high	4 minutes
16 ounces	medium high	5 minutes
28 ounces	medium high	6 minutes

Note: Cooking times are for 1 jar. Add 2 minutes for every additional jar.

6. Cool and store according to directions on pages 14–15.

Check the power of your microwave and adjust the setting if necessary (see page 9).

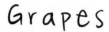

Grapes

INGREDIENTS

grapes

Medium Syrup (see page 12)

METHOD

1. Choose firm, unblemished grapes. Seedless sultana grapes are the most convenient to use. Wash fruit and remove any stalks. If using grapes with seeds, push rounded end of a sterilized bobby pin into hole left by stalk and pull out seeds.
2. Pack fruit into clean, sterilized jars.
3. Fill jars to overflowing with Medium Syrup. Fit lids on jars.
4. Cook according to the table below.

JAR SIZE	OVEN SETTING	COOKING TIME
8 ounces	medium high	3 minutes
16 ounces	medium high	5 minutes
28 ounces	medium high	8 minutes

Note: Cooking times are for 1 jar. Add 2 minutes for every additional jar.

5. Cool and store according to directions on pages 14–15.

Check the power of your microwave and adjust the setting if necessary (see page 9).

Honey Brandy Grapes

INGREDIENTS

grapes
1 tablespoon honey for every 1 cup of syrup
1 tablespoon brandy for every 1 cup of syrup
Medium Syrup (see page 12)

METHOD

1. Choose firm, unblemished grapes. Seedless sultana grapes are the most convenient to use. Wash fruit and remove any stalks. If using grapes with seeds, push rounded end of a sterilized bobby pin into hole left by stalk and pull out seeds.
2. Pack fruit into clean, sterilized jar.
3. Stir honey and brandy into warm Medium Syrup.
4. Fill jars to overflowing with syrup. Fit lids on jars.
5. Cook according to table below.

JAR SIZE	OVEN SETTING	COOKING TIME
8 ounces	medium high	3 minutes
16 ounces	medium high	5 minutes
28 ounces	medium high	8 minutes

Note: Cooking times are for 1 jar. Add 2 minutes for every additional jar.

6. Cool and store according to directions on pages 14–15.

Check the power of your microwave and adjust the setting if necessary (see page 9).

Guava

INGREDIENTS

12–15 guavas

1–2 cups Medium Syrup (see page 12)

1 teaspoon lemon juice per cup of fruit

METHOD

1. Wash and peel fruit, cut in half lengthwise.
2. Fill clean sterilized jars with fruit, add 1 teaspoon of lemon juice to each cup of fruit, cover fruit with syrup. Fit lids on jars.
3. Cook according to table below.

JAR SIZE	OVEN SETTING	COOKING TIME
8 ounces	medium high	3 minutes
16 ounces	medium high	5 minutes
28 ounces	medium high	7 minutes

Note: Cooking times are for 1 jar. Add 2 minutes for every additional jar.

4. Cool and store according to directions on pages 14–15.

Check the power of your microwave and adjust the setting if necessary (see page 9).

Loquats

INGREDIENTS

20–30 loquats

3–4 cups Medium Syrup (see page 12)

2 teaspoons lemon juice to every cup of syrup

METHOD

1. Wash loquats, remove bottom or blossom end, peel.
2. Pack loquats into clean sterilized jars. Cover with syrup to overflowing. Fit lids on jars.
3. Cook according to table below.

JAR SIZE	OVEN SETTING	COOKING TIME
8 ounces	medium high	3 minutes
16 ounces	medium high	5 minutes
28 ounces	medium high	7 minutes

Note: Cooking times are for 1 jar. Add 2 minutes for every additional jar.

4. Cool and store according to directions on pages 14–15.

Check the power of your microwave and adjust the setting if necessary (see page 9).

Lychees

INGREDIENTS

16 ozs lychees

3–4 cups Light Syrup (see page 12)

3 teaspoons citric acid to every 4 cups syrup

METHOD

1. Prepare lychees, by piercing shell at tip end with a small sharp knife, cut back to stem end on both sides. Discard shell.
2. Add citric acid to syrup.
3. Place lychees into hot syrup and allow to stand 30 minutes or until syrup is cool.
4. Remove lychees from syrup and fill clean sterilized jars. Pour syrup over lychees to overflowing. Fit lids on jars.
5. Cook according to table below.

JAR SIZE	OVEN SETTING	COOKING TIME
8 ounces	medium high	3 minutes
16 ounces	medium high	4 minutes
28 ounces	medium high	5 minutes

Note: Cooking times are for 1 jar. Add 2 minutes for every additional jar.

6. Cool and store according to directions on pages 14–15.

Check the power of your microwave and adjust the setting if necessary (see page 9).

Mandarins

INGREDIENTS

mandarins

Medium Syrup (see page 12)

METHOD

1. Choose fresh, ripe, unblemished fruit. Peel, divide into segments and remove stringy pith. Strip skin away from each segment and remove any seeds.
2. Pack fruit into clean, sterilized jars.
3. Fill jars to overflowing with Medium Syrup. Fit lids on jars.
4. Cook according to table below.

JAR SIZE	OVEN SETTING	COOKING TIME
8 ounces	medium high	3 minutes
16 ounces	medium high	5 minutes
28 ounces	medium high	8 minutes

Note: Cooking times are for 1 jar. Add 2 minutes for every additional jar.

5. Cool and store according to directions on pages 14–15.

Check the power of your microwave and adjust the setting if necessary (see page 9).

Orange Segments

INGREDIENTS

oranges

Medium Syrup (see page 12)

METHOD

1. Peel oranges and remove pith. Divide into segments, strip skin away from each segment and remove any seeds.
2. Pack fruit into clean, sterilized jars.
3. Fill jars to overflowing with Medium Syrup. Fit lids on jars.
4. Cook according to table below.

JAR SIZE	OVEN SETTING	COOKING TIME
8 ounces	medium high	3 minutes
16 ounces	medium high	5 minutes
28 ounces	medium high	8 minutes

Note: Cooking times are for 1 jar. Add 2 minutes for every additional jar.

5. Cool and store according to directions on pages 14–15.

Check the power of your microwave and adjust the setting if necessary (see page 9).

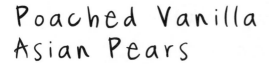

Poached Vanilla Asian Pears

INGREDIENTS

1½ Asian pears

1 cup dry white wine

½ teaspoon vanilla extract

3 tablespoons sugar

2 tablespoons lemon juice

METHOD

1. Heat wine, lemon juice, and sugar to boiling point on HIGH, for about 2–3 minutes.
2. Stir to dissolve sugar. Cool, add vanilla.
3. Peel pears, cut in halves, remove core, cut large pears into quarters.
4. Pack fruit into clean sterilized jars, cover fruit with syrup. Fit lids on jars.
5. Cook according to table below.

JAR SIZE	OVEN SETTING	COOKING TIME
8 ounces	medium high	3 minutes
16 ounces	medium high	5 minutes
28 ounces	medium high	7 minutes

Note: Cooking times are for 1 jar. Add 2 minutes for every additional jar.

6. Cool and store according to directions on pages 14–15.

Check the power of your microwave and adjust the setting if necessary (see page 9).

Pawpaw (Papaya) with Curacao

INGREDIENTS

1 small ripe pawpaw (papaya)

4 tablespoons sugar

1 teaspoon water

½ teaspoon citric acid

¾ cup white Curacao

METHOD

1. Peel pawpaws, cut in half and scoop out seed. Cut into slices or cubes.
2. Pack fruit into clean, sterilized jars.
3. Place sugar and water in a microwave-proof bowl and cook on HIGH for 1 minute, or until sugar dissolves. Cool, add citric acid and Curacao and stir.
4. Fill jars to overflowing with syrup. Fit lids on jars.
5. Cook according to table below.

JAR SIZE	OVEN SETTING	COOKING TIME
8 ounces	medium high	4 minutes
16 ounces	medium high	5 minutes
28 ounces	medium high	6 minutes

Note: Cooking times are for 1 jar. Add 2 minutes for every additional jar.

6. Cool and store according to directions on pages 14–15.

Check the power of your microwave and adjust the setting if necessary (see page 9).

Peaches
(Clingstone and Freestone)

INGREDIENTS

peaches

Medium Syrup (see page 12)

METHOD

1. Peel peaches with a stainless steel knife or peeling utensil. Alternatively, immerse peaches in boiling water for 2 minutes, then dip in cold water and pull off skins.
2. Leave fruit whole, or halve or slice. To remove stones from clingstone peaches, insert a round-bladed knife or a peach-pitting spoon at stalk end, and cut flesh away from stone. To remove stones from freestone peaches, cut around natural line of fruit and twist apart.
3. Pack fruit into clean, sterilized jars.
4. Fill jars to overflowing with Medium Syrup. Fit lids on jars.
5. Cook according to table below.

JAR SIZE	OVEN SETTING	COOKING TIME
8 ounces	medium high	5 minutes
16 ounces	medium high	8 minutes
28 ounces	medium high	12 minutes

Note: Cooking times are for 1 jar. Add 2 minutes for every additional jar.

6. Cool and store according to directions on pages 14–15.

Check the power of your microwave and adjust the setting if necessary (see page 9).

Pears

INGREDIENTS

pears

lemon strips

Medium Syrup (see page 12)

METHOD

1. Peel, core and cut pears in half. Immerse fruit in suggested solution to prevent discoloring (see page 14). When ready to use, drain pear pieces and rinse in fresh, cold water.
2. Pack fruit into clean, sterilized jars.
3. Fill jars to overflowing with Medium Syrup.
4. Add 2–3 lemon peel strips to every jar to enhance color and flavor while stored.
5. Fit lids on jars.
6. Cook according to table below.

JAR SIZE	OVEN SETTING	COOKING TIME
8 ounces	medium high	5 minutes
16 ounces	medium high	8 minutes
28 ounces	medium high	12 minutes

Note: Cooking times are for 1 jar. Add 2 minutes for every additional jar.

7. Cool and store according to directions on pages 14–15.

Check the power of your microwave and adjust the setting if necessary (see page 9).

Pears with Green Ginger

INGREDIENTS

pears

2 ozs green ginger for every 3–4 pears

Medium Syrup (see page 12)

METHOD

1. Peel, core and cut pears in half. Immerse fruit in suggested solution to prevent discoloring (see page 14). When ready to use, drain pear pieces and rinse in fresh, cold water.
2. Peel ginger, cut into thin slices and cook in 1 cup of water on HIGH until tender (about 6–8 minutes).
3. Pack fruit and ginger into clean, sterilized jars.
4. Fill jars to overflowing with Medium Syrup. Fit lids on jars.
5. Cook according to table below.

JAR SIZE	OVEN SETTING	COOKING TIME
8 ounces	medium high	5 minutes
16 ounces	medium high	8 minutes
28 ounces	medium high	12 minutes

Note: Cooking times are for 1 jar. Add 2 minutes for every additional jar.

6. Cool and store according to directions on pages 14–15.

Check the power of your microwave and adjust the setting if necessary (see page 9).

Poached Vanilla Pears

INGREDIENTS

pears

1 cup dry white wine

½ teaspoon vanilla extract

2 tablespoons sugar

2 tablespoons lemon juice

METHOD

1. Heat wine, lemon juice, and sugar to boiling point on HIGH. Stir to dissolve sugar, add vanilla.
2. Peel pears, cut in halves, remove core.
3. Immerse in suggested solution (see page 14). When ready to use, drain pears and rinse in fresh cold water.
4. Place into clean sterilized jars. Pour in enough wine syrup to half fill. Fit lids on jars.
5. Cook according to table below.

JAR SIZE	OVEN SETTING	COOKING TIME
8 ounces	medium high	2 minutes
16 ounces	medium high	3 minutes
28 ounces	medium high	5 minutes

Note: Cooking times are for 1 jar. Add 1 minute for every additional jar.

6. Cool and store according to directions on pages 14–15.

Check the power of your microwave and adjust the setting if necessary (see page 9).

Pineapple

INGREDIENTS

pineapple

Medium Syrup (see page 12)

METHOD

1. Peel, eye, and core pineapple. Cut into cubes, wedges or circles.
2. Pack fruit into clean, sterilized jars.
3. Fill jars to overflowing with Medium Syrup. Fit lids on jars.
4. Cook according to table below.

JAR SIZE	OVEN SETTING	COOKING TIME
8 ounces	medium high	5 minutes
16 ounces	medium high	8 minutes
28 ounces	medium high	12 minutes

Note: Cooking times are for 1 jar. Add 2 minutes for every additional jar.

5. Cool and store according to directions on pages 14–15.

Check the power of your microwave and adjust the setting if necessary (see page 69).

Pineapple and Passionfruit

INGREDIENTS

1 pineapple

4–6 passionfruit

Medium Syrup (see page 12)

METHOD

1. Peel, eye, and core pineapple. Cut into cubes, wedges or circles. Remove pulp from passionfruit and stir into pineapple pieces.
2. Pack fruit into clean, sterilized jars.
3. Fill jars to overflowing with Medium Syrup. Fit lids on jars.
4. Cook according to table below.

JAR SIZE	OVEN SETTING	COOKING TIME
8 ounces	medium high	5 minutes
16 ounces	medium high	8 minutes
28 ounces	medium high	12 minutes

Note: Cooking times are for 1 jar. Add 2 minutes for every additional jar.

5. Cool and store according to directions on pages 14–15.

Check the power of your microwave and adjust the setting if necessary (see page 9).

Plums

INGREDIENTS

plums

Medium Syrup (see page 12)

METHOD

1. When using whole plums wash and prick all over with a sterilized needle to prevent skins from splitting when cooked. Cut around the natural line of the fruit and twist halves apart. Remove and discard stone.
2. Pack fruit into clean, sterilized jars.
3. Fill jars to overflowing with Medium Syrup. Fit lids on jars.
4. Cook according to table below.

JAR SIZE	OVEN SETTING	COOKING TIME
8 ounces	medium high	5 minutes
16 ounces	medium high	8 minutes
28 ounces	medium high	12 minutes

Note: Cooking times are for 1 jar. Add 2 minutes for every additional jar.

5. Cool and store according to directions on pages 14–15.

Check the power of your microwave and adjust the setting if necessary (see page 9).

Quinces

INGREDIENTS

quinces

Heavy Syrup

METHOD

1. Peel, core, and quarter quinces, then slice or dice. If not using immediately, immerse fruit in solution to prevent discoloration (see page 14). When ready to serve, drain and rinse in fresh, cold water.
2. Place quinces and Heavy Syrup in a microwave-proof bowl and cook on MEDIUM HIGH at boiling point for 4–5 minutes. Cool.
3. Pack fruit into clean, sterilized jars.
4. Fill jars to overflowing with Heavy Syrup. Fit lids on jars.
5. Cook according to table below.

JAR SIZE	OVEN SETTING	COOKING TIME
8 ounces	medium high	3 minutes
16 ounces	medium high	4 minutes
28 ounces	medium high	5 minutes

Note: Cooking times are for 1 jar. Add 2 minutes for every additional jar.

6. Cool and store according to directions on pages 14–15.

Check the power of your microwave and adjust the setting if necessary (see page 9).

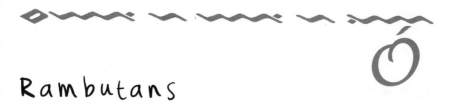

Rambutans

INGREDIENTS

20–24 rambutans

3–4 cups Light Syrup

2 teaspoons of citric acid to every cup of syrup

METHOD

1. Prepare rambutans by cutting away top or stem. Peel back skin and discard.
2. Fill clean sterilized jars with rambutans. Cover with syrup to overflowing. Fit lids on jars.
3. Cook according to table below.

JAR SIZE	OVEN SETTING	COOKING TIME
8 ounces	medium high	3 minutes
16 ounces	medium high	5 minutes
28 ounces	medium high	7 minutes

Note: Cooking times are for 1 jar. Add 2 minutes for every additional jar.

4. Cool and store according to directions on pages 14–15.

Check the power of your microwave and adjust the setting if necessary (see page 9).

Rhubarb

INGREDIENTS

rhubarb

Heavy Syrup

METHOD

1. Choose young, tender rhubarb stalks.
2. Trim away base and leaves, and cut stalks into 1½ inch lengths.
3. Pack stalks into clean, sterilized jars.
4. Fill jars to overflowing with Heavy Syrup. Fit lids on jars.
5. Cook according to table below.

JAR SIZE	OVEN SETTING	COOKING TIME
8 ounces	medium high	5 minutes
16 ounces	medium high	8 minutes
28 ounces	medium high	12 minutes

Note: Cooking times are for 1 jar. Add 2 minutes for every additional jar.

6. Cool and store according to directions on pages 14–15.

Check the power of your microwave and adjust the setting if necessary (see page 9).

Tomato Pulp

INGREDIENTS

tomatoes

brine (1 oz salt for every 3 cups of water)

METHOD

1. Immerse tomatoes in boiling water for 2–3 minutes, then place in cold water and peel off skins.
2. Cut up tomatoes roughly.
3. Pack fruit into clean, sterilized jars.
4. Fill jars to overflowing with brine. Fit lids on jars.
5. Cook according to table below.

JAR SIZE	OVEN SETTING	COOKING TIME
8 ounces	medium high	5 minutes
16 ounces	medium high	8 minutes
28 ounces	medium high	12 minutes

Note: Cooking times are for 1 jar. Add 2 minutes for every additional jar.

6. Repeat Step 5 on following day.
7. Cool and store according to directions on pages 14–15.

Check the power of your microwave and adjust the setting if necessary (see page 9).

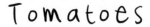

Tomatoes

INGREDIENTS

small whole tomatoes, or halves

brine (1 oz salt for every 3 cups of water)

METHOD

1. Immerse tomatoes in boiling water for 2–3 minutes, then place in cold water and peel off skins.
2. Pack fruit into clean, sterilized jars.
3. Fill jars to overflowing with brine. Fit lids on jars.
4. Cook according to table below.

JAR SIZE	OVEN SETTING	COOKING TIME
8 ounces	medium high	5 minutes
16 ounces	medium high	8 minutes
28 ounces	medium high	12 minutes

Note: Cooking times are for 1 jar. Add 2 minutes for every additional jar.

5. Repeat Step 4 on following day.
6. Cool and store according to directions on pages 14–15.

Check the power of your microwave and adjust the setting if necessary (see page 9).

Two Fruits

INGREDIENTS
Suggested combinations:
peach and pear,
peach and apricot,
pineapple and apricot,
berry and diced apple,
quince and apple
Medium Syrup (see page 12)

METHOD
1. Choose ripe, unblemished fruit and prepare as required.
2. Pack fruit into clean, sterilized jars.
3. Fill jars to overflowing with Medium Syrup. Fit lids on jars.
4. Cook according to table below.

JAR SIZE	OVEN SETTING	COOKING TIME
8 ounces	medium high	5 minutes
16 ounces	medium high	8 minutes
28 ounces	medium high	12 minutes

Note: Cooking times are for 1 jar. Add 2 minutes for every additional jar.

5. Cool and store according to directions on pages 14–15.

Note: do not use fruit low in citric acid, such as bananas, cantaloupe, figs, pawpaw or mango. These fruits may be added on serving.

Check the power of your microwave and adjust the setting if necessary (see page 9).

3

"Just Fruit" Canning

I call this type of canning "Just Fruit" because the only thing to go in the jar is the fruit itself – *nothing else*! Think what a boon this is for weight-watchers. Because fruit has such a high water content, it can be preserved in the microwave with no additives, not even water. What could be easier? The microwave acts very quickly on the fruit juices to create the temperature required to preserve (180°F). Excess air will be expelled on heating, so partly filled jars do not present a problem. During cooking, fruit juice will appear, and the fruit will hold its shape. However, if more juice is required, cover the base of the jar with one inch of cold water before adding the fruit. You can use this method to preserve a single piece of fruit, a full jar of fruit or even half a jar.

Some of you may prefer to add a small amount of sugar, honey, or molasses to the fruit (see next page). It's up to you.

The "Just Fruit" method is ideal for a single serve, a special diet or simply a change. "Just Fruit", served with a topping or ice-cream, makes a mouth-watering, nourishing dessert for children.

Alternative Sweeteners

With the "Just Fruit" method of canning, sweeteners may be added to the fruit in the jar before preserving, or the fruit may be sweetened to taste on serving. If added before preserving, the sweetener might not dissolve immediately, but it will do so after standing for a while. The following quantities are suggested:

granulated sugar – 1 dessertspoon per cup of fruit

honey or light molasses – 1 tablespoon per cup of fruit

artificial sweeteners – Add to taste. These are best added on serving because cooking and storage can cause bitterness. Once opened, any left-over fruit that has been artificially sweetened must be kept refrigerated.

Just Apples
(circles, diced or quarters)

METHOD

1. Choose firm, ripe, unblemished apples. Peel and core, then dice, slice or quarter. Immerse fruit in suggested solution to prevent discoloration (see page 14).
2. Place in clean, sterilized jars. Add sweetener if desired.
3. Fit lids on jars.
4. Cook as follows:

FRUIT	JAR SIZE	OVEN SETTING	COOKING TIME
1 apple	8 ounces	medium high	2 minutes
2–3 apples	16 ounces	medium high	3 minutes

Note: Cooking times are for 1 jar. Add 1 minute for every additional jar.

5. Cool and store as directed on pages 14–15.

Check the power of your microwave and adjust the setting if necessary (see page 9).

Just Apricots
(whole or halves)

METHOD

1. Choose firm, ripe, unblemished apricots. Use whole, or halve by cutting around the natural line with a stainless steel knife. Twist halves apart and remove and discard stones. Immerse fruit in suggested solution to prevent discoloration (see page 14).
2. Place in clean, sterilized jars with cut side facing down, and overlapping. Add sweetener if desired.
3. Fit lids on jars.
4. Cook according to table below.

FRUIT	JAR SIZE	OVEN SETTING	COOKING TIME
4–5 apricots	8 ounces	medium high	2 minutes
8–12 apricots	16 ounces	medium high	3 minutes
20–25 apricots	28 ounces	medium high	5 minutes

Note: Cooking times are for 1 jar. Add 1 minute for every additional jar.

5. Cool and store as directed on pages 14–15.

Check the power of your microwave and adjust the setting if necessary (see page 9).

Just Berries

This method is suitable for most berries, including strawberries, raspberries, loganberries, and blackberries.

METHOD

1. Choose full, ripe berries, making sure they are unblemished. Wash, and remove any stems.
2. Place berries in a microwave-proof bowl. Add sweetener if desired.
3. Cook on HIGH for 1 minute. Remove from oven and allow to stand until cool.
4. Place in clean, sterilized jars.
5. Fit lids on jars.
6. Cook according to table below.

FRUIT	JAR SIZE	OVEN SETTING	COOKING TIME
1 cup	8 ounces	medium high	1 minute
2 cups	16 ounces	medium high	2 minutes
3 cups	28 ounces	medium high	4 minutes

Note: Cooking times are for 1 jar. Add 1 minute for every additional jar.

7. Cool and store according to directions on pages 14–15.

Check the power of your microwave and adjust the setting if necessary (see page 9).

Just Cantaloupe
(balls or diced)

METHOD

1. Choose a firm, ripe cantaloupe.
2. Peel and seed fruit. With a melon-baller, scoop out small balls, or slice or dice.
3. Place in clean sterilized jars. Add sweetener if desired.
4. For each cup of fruit add ½ teaspoon citric acid.
5. Fit lids on jars.
6. Cook according to table below.

FRUIT	JAR SIZE	OVEN SETTING	COOKING TIME
1 cup	8 ounces	medium high	2 minutes
2 cups	16 ounces	medium high	3 minutes
3 cups	28 ounces	medium high	5 minutes

Note: Cooking times are for 1 jar. Add 1 minute for every additional jar.

7. Cool and store according to directions on pages 14–15.

Check the power of your microwave and adjust the setting if necessary (see page 9).

Just Cherries

METHOD

1. Choose ripe, unblemished cherries and wash well.
   Stone fruit with cherry-stoner if desired.
2. Place fruit in clean, sterilized jars. Add sweetener if desired.
3. Fit lids on jars.
4. Cook according to table below.

FRUIT	JAR SIZE	OVEN SETTING	COOKING TIME
1 cup	8 ounces	medium high	2 minutes
2 cups	16 ounces	medium high	3 minutes
3 cups	28 ounces	medium high	5 minutes

Note: Cooking times are for 1 jar. Add 1 minute for every additional jar.

5. Cool and store according to directions on pages 14–15.

Check the power of your microwave and adjust the setting if necessary (see page 9).

Just Cherry Plums

METHOD

1. Choose ripe, unblemished cherry plums and wash well.
2. Place fruit in clean, sterilized jars. Add sweetener if desired.
3. Fit lids on jars.
4. Cook according to table below.

FRUIT	JAR SIZE	OVEN SETTING	COOKING TIME
1 cup	8 ounces	medium high	2 minutes
2 cups	16 ounces	medium high	3 minutes
3 cups	28 ounces	medium high	5 minutes

Note: Cooking times are for 1 jar. Add 1 minute for every additional jar.

5. Cool and store according to directions on pages 14–15.

Check the power of your microwave and adjust the setting if necessary (see page 9).

Just Citrus Fruit
(Grapefruit, oranges, mandarins)

METHOD

1. Choose unblemished fruit.
2. Peel, taking away all the pith, and remove segments by cutting down to center of the fruit on each side of the segment's dividing line. Slip the knife in at the bottom of each segment and push it free. Set aside, ready for canning.
3. Place in clean, sterilized jars. Add sweetener if desired.
4. Fit lids on jars.
5. Cook according to table below.

FRUIT	JAR SIZE	OVEN SETTING	COOKING TIME
1 cup	8 ounces	medium high	2 minutes
2 cups	16 ounces	medium high	3 minutes
3 cups	28 ounces	medium high	4 minutes

Note: Cooking times are for 1 jar. Add 1 minute for every additional jar.

6. Cool and store according to directions on pages 14–15.

Check the power of your microwave and adjust the setting if necessary (see page 9).

Just Fruit Salad

METHOD

1. Selection of fruits is important. Fruits low in natural acids are not recommended, e.g. bananas, cantaloupe, pawpaw, figs, and mangoes, but these can be preserved separately (with citric acid) and added just before serving. The most common fruits used are: apples, apricots, cherries, grapes, pineapple, peaches, and oranges.
2. Peel if necessary. Cut or dice.
3. Mix all fruits together. Add sweetener if desired.
4. Place in clean, sterilized jars.
5. Fit lids on jars.
6. Cook according to table below.

FRUIT	JAR SIZE	OVEN SETTING	COOKING TIME
1 cup	8 ounces	medium high	2 minutes
2 cups	16 ounces	medium high	3 minutes
3 cups	28 ounces	medium high	5 minutes

Note: Cooking times are for 1 jar. Add 1 minute for every additional jar.

7. Cool and store according to directions on pages 14–15.

Check the power of your microwave and adjust the setting if necessary (see page 9).

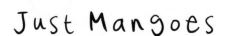

Just Mangoes

METHOD

1. Skin mangoes by peeling down from stem. The skin will come away easily if the fruit is ripe.
2. Cut flesh from seed and slice into wedges or pieces.
3. Place in clean, sterilized jars. Add sweetener if desired.
4. For each cup of fruit add ½ teaspoon citric acid.
5. Fit lids on jars.
6. Cook according to table below.

FRUIT	JAR SIZE	OVEN SETTING	COOKING TIME
1 mango	8 ounces	medium high	2 minutes
2 mangoes	16 ounces	medium high	3 minutes
3 mangoes	28 ounces	medium high	4 minutes

Note: Cooking times are for 1 jar. Add 1 minute for every additional jar.

7. Cool and store according to directions on pages 14–15.

Check the power of your microwave and adjust the setting if necessary (see page 9).

Just Persimmons

METHOD

1. Cut persimmons into halves, scoop out flesh into a bowl. Add sugar to taste if desired.
2. Fill clean sterilized jars to about 1½ inches from the top of jar.
3. Fit lids on jars.
4. Cook according to table below.

FRUIT	JAR SIZE	OVEN SETTING	COOKING TIME
1 cup	8 ounces	medium high	2 minutes
2 cups	16 ounces	medium high	3 minutes
3 cups	28 ounces	medium high	5 minutes

Note: Cooking times are for 1 jar. Add 1 minute for every additional jar.

5. Cool and store according to directions on pages 14–15.

Check the power of your microwave and adjust the setting if necessary (see page 9).

Just Pineapple
(wedges, circles or diced)

METHOD

1. Peel, eye, and core pineapple.
2. Cut into wedges, circles or dice.
3. Place in clean, sterilized jars. Add sweetener if desired.
4. Fit lids on jars.
5. Cook according to table below.

FRUIT	JAR SIZE	OVEN SETTING	COOKING TIME
1 cup	8 ounces	medium high	2 minutes
2 cups	16 ounces	medium high	3 minutes
3 cups	28 ounces	medium high	5 minutes

Note: Cooking times are for 1 jar. Add 1 minute for every additional jar.

6. Cool and store according to directions on pages 14–15.

Check the power of your microwave and adjust the setting if necessary (see page 9).

Just Plums

METHOD

1. Choose firm, ripe, unblemished plums and wash well. Use whole, or halve by cutting around the natural line with a stainless steel knife. Twist halves apart, remove, and discard stones.
2. If preserving whole, prick plums all over with a sterilized needle or skewer to prevent the skins from splitting while cooking.
3. Place in clean, sterilized jars, with cut side facing down and overlapping (if halved). Add sweetener if desired.
4. Fit lids on jars.
5. Cook according to table below.

FRUIT	JAR SIZE	OVEN SETTING	COOKING TIME
1 cup	8 ounces	medium high	2 minutes
2 cups	16 ounces	medium high	3 minutes
3 cups	28 ounces	medium high	5 minutes

Note: Cooking times are for 1 jar. Add 1 minute for every additional jar.

6. Cool and store according to directions on pages 14–15.

Check the power of your microwave and adjust the setting if necessary (see page 9).

Just Tomatoes

METHOD

1. Tomatoes may be peeled by immersing them in boiling water for 2–3 minutes first. The skins will then come away easily.
2. Cut tomatoes up roughly and place in clean, sterilized jars.
3. Fit lids on jars.
4. Cook according to table below.

FRUIT	JAR SIZE	OVEN SETTING	COOKING TIME
1 cup	8 ounces	medium high	2 minutes
2 cups	16 ounces	medium high	3 minutes
3 cups	28 ounces	medium high	5 minutes

Note: Cooking times are for 1 jar. Add 1 minute for every additional jar.

5. Cool for 12 hours then repeat Step 5 without loosening screw-on lids or removing spring clips.
6. Cool and store according to directions on pages 14–15.

Check the power of your microwave and adjust the setting if necessary (see page 6).

4

Preserves, Marmalades, Jellies, and Conserves

Preserves, marmalades, jellies, and conserves can be made quickly, easily and economically in the microwave oven. The process enhances the taste and color of the fruit.

You don't need a large amount of fruit for this method. In fact, about 4 to 5 lbs is an ideal quantity for the best results. Any more than this amount tends to negate the time-saving and other benefits of the microwave method.

Preserve made in the microwave is delicious as it has the full fruit flavor. Very little or no water is needed, as the microwave draws out the natural fruit juices, and so the fruit is more concentrated. An added bonus is that less sugar is needed for setting.

It is impossible to give exact cooking times – the type of fruit used, its condition and degree of ripeness will determine the cooking times. The times given here are as accurate as possible. If you follow the method and test the mixture when you think it is ready, you should achieve good results.

Equipment

All types of preserves, marmalades, jellies, and conserves require the same simple equipment.

1. large, microwave-proof bowl with a cover
2. large spoon, preferably wooden
3. clean jars, free of chips, ridges or other imperfections, and sufficient cover or screw-top lids to fit

Sterilizing the Equipment

1. Check that the jars you intend to use will fit in your microwave oven with their lids on.
2. Half-fill jars with water, place in oven and cook on HIGH until water boils (about two minutes for each jar).
3. Remove jars from oven and pour away water. Any excess water will evaporate as the jars cool.

Testing for Setting Point

It is essential to test mixtures to make sure that the setting point has been reached; otherwise the product will be runny and unusable. The following steps are common to all preserves, marmalades, jellies, and conserves.

1. Before preparing fruit, place a saucer in the refrigerator (see Step 3).
2. Remove the bowl of cooked preserve from the microwave while you test it. (If you continue cooking fruit while testing a sample, it may be cooked beyond setting point, spoiling the flavor, texture, and color of the final product.)
3. Put a teaspoon of the hot mixture on the chilled saucer and cool. When cool, the surface should crinkle when the saucer is tilted slightly.
4. If the test is not positive, return the bowl to microwave and cook on HIGH for a few more minutes. Then repeat this test.

Vacuum Sealing

Vacuum sealing expels the air from filled jars and seals them. While it is not essential to vacuum seal preserves, the process will ensure the longest possible keeping time.

1. Choose screw-top jars with built-in sealing rings or inserts.
2. After you fill the jars, screw on lids.
3. While filled jars are still warm, place them in microwave, about 1¼ apart, and cook on MEDIUM HIGH for 1 to 2 minutes. Remove jars from the microwave and place on a towel, several sheets of newspaper or a chopping board to prevent cracking.
4. When cool, the lids will be slightly concave, showing that a vacuum seal has been achieved.

Storage

Store preserves, marmalades, jellies, and conserves in a cool, dark place. This retards the growth of mold. If mold does form, remove and discard. Place remaining mixture in a microwave-proof bowl and cook on HIGH at boiling point for 2 to 3 minutes. Re-bottle in clean, warm jars and vacuum seal.

Pectin and Fruit Acids

Pectin, a naturally occurring fruit acid, is a vital element in preserves, marmalades, jellies, and conserves. Without pectin, they would not set. The highest quantities of pectin occur in fruits that are firm and just under-ripe (pectin in overripe fruit converts to sugar).

Fruits that have high levels of acid are ideal, as the acid inhibits the growth of bacteria and prevents the formation of toxins. Natural fruit acids are also necessary because they draw out pectin, improve the flavor of the fruit and help prevent crystallization. If the fruit is overripe, or naturally low in pectin or other fruit acids, lemon juice or citric acid must be added. The amounts required are specified in the recipes.

Sugar

White granulated sugar is the most popular variety used to make preserves, marmalades, jellies, and conserves. Sugar cubes can be used, but it is difficult to measure the correct proportion of sugar to fruit. Preserve can crystallize if too much sugar is used, or if sugar isn't dissolved fully before mixture boils.

Brown sugar can be used but it makes the fruit darker, so it should be used only for darker colored fruits such as plums or blackcurrants.

Fruits with high or moderate pectin content (see below) require equal amounts of sugar and fruit pulp, e.g. 1 cup of sugar to 1 cup of fruit.

Fruits with low pectin content require ¾ the amount of sugar to fruit pulp, e.g. ¾ cup of sugar to one cup of fruit.

The following tables will help you determine the proportion of sugar to fruit pulp to use when making preserves, marmalades, jellies, and conserves with fresh fruit.

Sugar Ratios

SUGAR REQUIRED FOR HIGH- AND MEDIUM- PECTIN FRUITS

SUGAR	FRUIT PULP
1 cup	1 cup
2 cups	2 cups
3 cups	3 cups

SUGAR REQUIRED FOR LOW- PECTIN FRUITS

SUGAR	FRUIT PULP
1½ cups	2 cups
2¼ cups	3 cups
3 cups	4 cups

HIGH-PECTIN FRUITS	MEDIUM-PECTIN FRUITS	LOW-PECTIN FRUITS
Cooking apples	Bananas	Apricots
Crab-apples	Ripe cherries	Blackberries
Quinces	Figs	Under-ripe cherries
Citrus fruits	Grapes	Loganberries
(cumquats,	Peaches	Greengage plums
grapefruits,	Pears	Ripe plums
lemons,	Strawberries	Pineapples
oranges)	Rhubarb	

Testing Pectin Content

Place a teaspoon of cooked or preserved fruit in three teaspoons of denatured alcohol and leave for 2 minutes until mixture clots and becomes firm.

Large, firm clots indicate high pectin content. Medium-sized clots which are not so firm indicate medium pectin content. Weak, flabby clots indicate low pectin content.

Overcoming Pectin Deficiency

Sweet, overripe fruits and fruits low in pectin can be used in preserves, marmalades, jellies, and conserves if one of the following steps is taken:
1. Add 2 tablespoons of lemon juice to every kilogram (4 cups) of fruit.
2. Add 1 teaspoon of citric acid to every 2 lbs (4 cups) of fruit.
3. Add commercially produced pectin, following the manufacturer's directions.

PRESERVES

There's nothing quite so delicious as a full-fruit preserve, which is just what you get when preserve is made in the microwave. An added bonus is that you don't have to stand there stirring for half the cooking time. What a time saver! And perhaps best of all, it's goodbye to preserve burnt onto the bottom of the saucepan, which is what happens with the traditional method. Even after soaking overnight it always clings on. Once you've made preserve in the microwave you won't want to make it any other way!

METHOD

The following steps are standard for all preserves made with fresh fruits, but check the following recipes for minor variations.

1. Choose firm, unblemished fruit which is slightly under-ripe. Cut away and discard any bruised areas.
2. Wash fruit, peel if necessary, cut into halves and remove any pips or stones.
3. Add lemon juice, water or citric acid if required.
4. Place fruit mixture in a covered microwave-proof bowl, cook on HIGH until soft and pulpy.
5. Remove bowl from oven and stir in required amount of sweetener while pulp is still hot, making sure it is fully dissolved.
6. Return mixture to microwave and cook uncovered on HIGH for about 15–20 minutes, until setting point has been reached (see page 70).
7. Skim preserve to remove any scum.
8. Fill clean, warm, sterilized jars to the brim.
9. Vacuum seal according to directions on page 71.
10. Label and date jars.
11. Cool and store according to direction on page 71.

Apple and Blackberry Preserve

INGREDIENTS

2 lbs cooking apples

2 lbs blackberries

3 cups honey

   (**or** *3 cups light molasses* **or** *2 lbs brown or white sugar*)

2 tablespoons lemon juice

   (**or** *1 teaspoon citric acid*)

METHOD

Follow directions on page 74.

Apple and Rhubarb Preserve

INGREDIENTS

1 lb cooking apples

1 lb rhubarb

1½ cups honey

   (or 1½ cups light molasses or 1 lb brown or white sugar)

2 tablespoons lemon juice

   (or 1 teaspoon citric acid)

METHOD

Follow directions on page 74.

Apricot Preserve

INGREDIENTS

2 lbs apricots

1½ cups honey

   (or 1½ cups light molasses or 1 lb brown or white sugar)

METHOD

Follow directions on page 74.

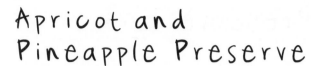

Apricot and Pineapple Preserve

INGREDIENTS

2 lbs apricots

2 cups drained crushed pineapple

1½ cups honey

   (*or* 1½ cups light molasses *or* 1 lb brown or white sugar)

METHOD

Follow directions on page 74.

Berry Preserve

INGREDIENTS

2 lbs raspberries

   (*or* 2 lbs blackberries *or* 2 lbs strawberries)

1½ cups honey

   (*or* 1½ cups light molasses *or* 1 lb brown or white sugar)

2 tablespoons lemon juice

   (*or* 1 teaspoon citric acid)

METHOD

Follow directions on page 74.

Cherry Preserve

INGREDIENTS
2 lbs cherries
1½ cups honey
   (**or** 1½ cups light molasses **or** 1 lb brown or white sugar)
2 tablespoons lemon juice
   (**or** 1 teaspoon citric acid)

METHOD
Follow directions on page 74.

Feijoa Preserve

INGREDIENTS
2 lbs feijoa
1¼ lbs sugar
½ cup water
2 tablespoons lemon juice
   (**or** 1 teaspoon citric acid)

METHOD
Peel and slice fruit. Follow directions on page 74.

Fig Preserve

INGREDIENTS
2 lbs figs
1½ cups honey
    *(**or** 1½ cups light molasses **or** 1 lb brown or white sugar)*
2 tablespoons lemon juice
    *(**or** 1 teaspoon citric acid)*

METHOD
Follow directions on page 74.

Fig and Ginger Preserve

INGREDIENTS
4 lbs figs
3 ozs fresh green ginger, bruised
3 cups honey
    *(**or** 3 cups light molasses **or** 2 lbs brown or white sugar)*
3 tablespoons lemon juice
    *(**or** 1½ teaspoons citric acid)*

METHOD
To bruise ginger, cut into small dice, then press firmly with the side
of the knife. Follow directions on page 74.

Guava Preserve

INGREDIENTS

2 lbs guavas

1¼ lbs sugar

3 tablespoons lemon juice
   (**or** 1½ teaspoons citric acid)

METHOD

Wash and peel guavas, chop up roughly. Follow directions on page 74.

Kiwifruit Preserve

INGREDIENTS

3 lbs kiwifruit

¾ cup water

1¼ lbs sugar

4 tablespoons lemon juice
   (**or** 2 teaspoons citric acid)

METHOD

Peel fruit and chop up roughly. Follow directions on page 74.

Loquat Preserve

INGREDIENTS

2 lbs loquats

1¼ lbs sugar

3 tablespoons lemon juice
   (*or* 1½ teaspoons citric acid)

METHOD

Choose loquats that are not overripe, remove seed, cut fruit up roughly. Follow directions on page 74.

Lychee Preserve

INGREDIENTS

2 lbs lychees

1¼ lbs sugar

3 tablespoons lemon juice
   (*or* 1½ teaspoons citric acid)

METHOD

Cover lychees with boiling water and soak for 10 minutes. Rub skins off and remove stone, cut fruit into quarters. Follow directions on page 74.

Persimmon Preserve

INGREDIENTS

3 lbs persimmons

1½ lbs sugar

2 tablespoons lemon juice
  (**or** 1 teaspoon citric acid)

METHOD

Cut persimmons in half, remove seeds, scoop out pulp, discard skins.
Blend fruit in a blender to a purée. Follow directions on page 74.

Pineapple Preserve

INGREDIENTS

2 lbs pineapple

1½ cups honey
  (**or** 1½ cups light molasses **or** 1 lb brown or white sugar)

2 tablespoons lemon juice
  (**or** 1 teaspoon citric acid)

METHOD

Follow directions on page 74.

Plum Preserve

INGREDIENTS

4 lbs plums
3 cups honey
   (or 3 cups light molasses or 2 lbs brown or white sugar)

METHOD
Follow directions on page 74.

Rhubarb Preserve

INGREDIENTS

2 lbs rhubarb
1¼ lbs sugar
¼ cup lemon juice

METHOD
Remove leaves and base of rhubarb, wash, cut into 2 inch pieces.
Follow directions on page 74.

Tamarillo Preserve

INGREDIENTS

2 lbs tamarillos

1¼ lbs cooking apples

24 ozs sugar

2 tablespoons lemon juice

(or 1 teaspoon citric acid)

METHOD

Immerse tamarillos in boiling water for 2–3 minutes, remove skins, cut tamarillos up roughly. Peel and core apples, grate finely. Follow directions on page 74.

CONSERVES

Conserves are simply preserves made with whole fruits, or with large pieces of fruit and are usually made from fruits with low pectin content. However, high-pectin fruits can also be used. Very little water is added, as this keeps the pectin concentrated, giving the conserve greater setting power. The following steps are standard for all conserves made with fresh fruits, but check the following recipes for minor variations.

METHOD

1. Wash fruit, remove stalks and blemishes, and cut in halves or quarters.
2. Place fruit, water, and lemon juice or citric acid in a large microwave-proof bowl and cook on HIGH until soft and pulpy (about 5–6 minutes).
3. Measure fruit pulp.
4. Reheat on HIGH to boiling point.
5. Stir in sugar until dissolved.
6. Return uncovered mixture to microwave and cook on HIGH for about 15–20 minutes until setting point has been reached (see page 70).
7. Fill clean, warm sterilized jars to brim with conserve.
8. Fit lids on jars.
9. Label and date jars.
10. Store in a cool, dark place.

Fig Conserve

INGREDIENTS
2 lbs figs
¾ cup water
2 tablespoons lemon juice
(**or** 1 teaspoon citric acid)
1 lb sugar

METHOD
Follow directions on page 85.

Peach Conserve

INGREDIENTS
2 lbs peaches
¾ cup water
2 tablespoons lemon juice
(**or** 1 teaspoon citric acid)
1 lb sugar

METHOD
Follow directions on page 85.

Strawberry Conserve

INGREDIENTS

2 lbs strawberries

½ cup water

2 tablespoons lemon juice
  *(**or** 1 teaspoon citric acid)*

1 lb sugar

METHOD

Follow directions on page 85.

JELLIES

Jellies make a delicious change from preserves. They are actually strained preserves without fruit pulp. Jellies are firm and well-flavored and have a clear, bright color.

Fruits with high pectin content are the most suitable for jelly making. However, fruits with low pectin content can be used if lemon juice or citric acid is added. For best results from the microwave method, use small quantities of fruit.

Equipment

A jelly bag is required to strain the juices away from the fruit pulp. They can be purchased, and are made of several layers of very fine material, such as cheese cloth, which are attached to a circular frame and stand. They are placed over a basin which catches the strained liquid. You can make your own jelly bag by tying several layers of cheese cloth to the legs of an upturned chair, or you can use a very fine strainer.

METHOD

The following steps are standard for all jellies made with fresh fruits, but check the following recipes for minor variations.

1. Wash fruit and chop roughly, leaving pips, cores and skins.
2. Place in a microwave-proof bowl and add water, cover.
3. Cook on HIGH to boiling point (about 6–8 minutes) or until soft and pulpy.
4. Pour into a clean jelly bag, or a fine strainer, and let stand until juice drips through (for several hours or overnight). Do not press or squeeze any fruit pulp into juice as this will cloud the jelly.
5. Reheat juice on HIGH to boiling point. Remove bowl from microwave and stir in an equal amount of sugar until dissolved. Add lemon juice or citric acid, if required.

6. Return uncovered mixture to microwave and cook on HIGH for about 15–20 minutes until setting point has been reached (see page 70).
7. Fill clean, warm, sterilized jars to brim with jelly.
8. Fit lids on jars immediately. Vacuum seal (see page 71).
9. Label and date jars.
10. Store in a cool, dark place.

Apple Jelly

INGREDIENTS
5 large cooking apples
2½ cups water
equal amounts of sugar and liquid

METHOD
Follow directions on page 88.

Blackberry Jelly

INGREDIENTS
2 lbs blackberries
1 cup water
equal amounts of sugar and liquid
3 tablespoons lemon juice
(or 1½ teaspoons citric acid)

METHOD
Follow directions on page 88.

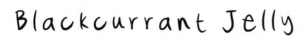

Blackcurrant Jelly

INGREDIENTS
2 lbs blackcurrants
1 cup water
equal amounts of sugar and liquid
2 tablespoons lemon juice
   (or 1½ teaspoons citric acid)

METHOD
Follow directions on page 88.

Crab Apple Jelly and Cranberry Jelly

INGREDIENTS
2 lbs crab apples
2 cups water
equal amounts of sugar and liquid
2 tablespoons lemon juice
   (or 1½ teaspoons citric acid)

METHOD
Follow direction on page 88.

Guava Jelly

INGREDIENTS
2 lbs guavas
2½ cups water
equal amounts of sugar and liquid
3 tablespoons lemon juice
(or 1½ teaspoons citric acid)

METHOD
Follow directions on page 88.

Quince Jelly

INGREDIENTS
2 lbs quinces
2½ cups water
equal amounts of sugar and liquid

METHOD
Follow directions on page 88.

MARMALADES

The following steps are standard for all marmalades made with fresh fruit, but check recipes for minor variations.

METHOD

1. Wash fruit and slice thinly.
2. Cover with water and let stand overnight, or for several hours.
3. Place fruit and water in a microwave-proof bowl, cover and cook on HIGH until rind is tender (about 6–10 minutes).
4. Strain to remove pips and rind. Retain desired amount of rind. Cut into fine (about half inch) strips. Add to strained mixture.
5. Measure strained mixture.
6. Reheat mixture on HIGH to boiling point. Stir in required amount of sugar until dissolved.
7. Return uncovered mixture to microwave and cook on HIGH for about 15 –20 minutes until setting point has been reached (see page 70).
8. Fill clean, warm, sterilized jars to brim with marmalade.
9. Fit lids on jars immediately. Do not allow marmalade to cool, as warm marmalade will create condensation, causing mold to grow.
10. Label and date jars.
11. Store in a cool dark place.

Breakfast Brandy Marmalade

INGREDIENTS

3 large oranges
2 large lemons
4 cups water
¼ cup brandy
equal amounts of sugar and pulp

METHOD
Follow directions on page 93.
Note: Add brandy at Step 2.

Ginger and Lemon Marmalade

INGREDIENTS

3 large lemons
½ cup preserved ginger, finely chopped
4 cups water
equal amounts sugar and pulp

METHOD
Follow directions on page 93.

Lime Marmalade

INGREDIENTS
8–10 limes
5 cups water
equal amounts of sugar and pulp

METHOD
Follow directions on page 93.

Orange Marmalade

INGREDIENTS
3 large oranges
¼ cup lemon juice
3 cups water
equal amounts of sugar and pulp

METHOD
Follow directions on page 93.

Note: Add lemon juice at Step 6.

Pineapple Marmalade

INGREDIENTS

3 cups fresh pineapple, finely chopped

2 oranges

1 lemon

4 cups water

equal amounts of sugar and pulp

METHOD

Follow directions on page 93.

Note: Allow ¾ cup of sugar for every cup of fruit.

Cook for 20–30 minutes to reach setting point.

Three Fruits Marmalade

INGREDIENTS

1 orange

1 lemon

1 grapefruit

4 cups water

equal amount of sugar and pulp

METHOD

Follow directions on page 93.

5

Pickles, Chutneys, and Relishes

It's very handy to have a few jars of pickles, chutneys, and relishes in the pantry to add to entrees and main courses. And they're great for adding a bit of zing to sandwiches or savories. For sugarless chutneys, see Chapter 6.

PICKLES

Making pickles in the microwave is very easy. They are made using mainly vegetables soaked in brine or sprinkled with salt. This process removes excess moisture, keeping the vegetable crisp, and prevents the formation of bacteria.

Vinegar

Vinegar is the preserving agent of pickles, sauces, and chutneys. The natural acids in vinegar prevent the growth of bacteria and fermentation. It is essential that a good quality vinegar is used. Malt vinegar (white or brown), a cider, or wine vinegar can also be used. Commercially produced spiced vinegar can be used, but a wider variety of flavors is possible if you prepare your own. The recipe is on page 99.

Spices

Whole spices should be used for pickles, as ground spices will make the vinegar cloudy. However, ground spices should be used for chutneys and relishes, as they give a stronger flavor. If you use whole spices for chutneys, add more than the amount stated in the recipe and tie them in a muslin bag. The bag can be removed easily before the chutney is bottled.

Brine

For best results use coarse cooking salt as refined table salt produces a cloudy effect. The ideal solution for soaking vegetables is ½ cup of salt to 8 cups water. Bring water to boiling point on HIGH, about 10–12 minutes. Dissolve the salt in the boiling water and cool. Strain the brine before using it, and carefully rinse all traces of it from the vegetables before soaking in spiced vinegar.

Sugar

Chutneys and relishes are usually sweetened with white granulated sugar, but brown sugar can be used to make the chutney or relish darker and alter the flavor.

Storing

Keep preserves in a cool cupboard for optimum flavor. Store for 2–4 weeks before using.

Spiced Vinegar

INGREDIENTS

1 pint vinegar

1 teaspoon whole cloves

2 teaspoons black peppercorns

2–3 bay leaves

2 inch piece cinnamon stick

1 teaspoon mustard seeds

METHOD

Place all ingredients in a microwave-proof bowl. Bring to boiling point on HIGH about 4–5 minutes. Allow to cool. Strain away spices, and pour spiced vinegar into clean bottles ready for use.

Artichoke Pickles

INGREDIENTS

1 lb jerusalem artichokes

3 medium onions

3 cups cider vinegar

½ cup sugar

3 teaspoons mustard powder

1 teaspoon turmeric

2 teaspoons mustard seeds

4–5 whole cloves

METHOD

1. Wash, peel and cut artichokes into small chunks. Peel and slice onions into rings. Place each into separate bowls, cover with cold water, add 2 tablespoons of salt to each bowl, mix gently. Stand for 12 hours or overnight.
2. Drain away all excess liquid from vegetables, rinse well in cold water, drain. Combine both vegetables and pack into clean jars.
3. Mix mustard powder, turmeric and a little vinegar into a thin paste. Place all remaining ingredients into a microwave bowl, stir in paste mixture.
4. Cook uncovered on HIGH to boiling point about 3–4 minutes, reduce power setting to MEDIUM HIGH and cook for a further 4–5 minutes. Pour hot liquid over artichokes and onion to cover.
5. Cover with a lid. Store to mature for 2–3 weeks before using.

Fruit Medley Pickles

INGREDIENTS

2–3 pears
1 cup pineapple pieces
1 cup sultana grapes
1 cup black grapes
2–3 cooking peaches
6–8 whole cloves
1 cup water
1 cup brown vinegar
1 cup sugar
1 tablespoon dry mustard
1 cinnamon stick

METHOD

1. Place water, vinegar, and sugar in a large microwave bowl, heat to boiling point on HIGH. Stir to dissolve sugar.
2. Peel pears and peaches, remove cores and stones. Cut fruits into quarters. Wash grapes and remove stems.
3. Place all fruits, mustard, and cloves into a bowl and mix well together.
4. Fill clean jars with fruit, add a small piece of cinnamon stick to each jar. Pour warm vinegar solution over to cover. Seal with a lid. Store.

Honey Walnuts

INGREDIENTS
½ lb walnut halves
½ cup honey
1 tablespoon lemon juice

METHOD
1. Place walnuts and honey into a microwave bowl. Cook on HIGH 2–3 minutes. Stir in lemon juice. Cool.
2. Fill clean jars with walnuts, cover with a lid. Use within 2–3 weeks.
3. To serve. Heat walnuts on HIGH for 1 minute. Serve with preserved fruit and/or ice cream.

Hot 'n' Spicy Tomato Pickle

INGREDIENTS

4 lbs tomatoes

1 cup sugar

½ cup fresh ginger, grated

10–12 green chilies

1½ cup brown sugar

6 garlic cloves, crushed

3 tablespoons ground cumin

1 tablespoon mustard seeds

1 tablespoon turmeric

1 tablespoon chili powder

1 teaspoon salt

METHOD

1. Soak mustard seeds in vinegar over night. Strain vinegar into another bowl to use later. Place garlic, ginger, and mustard seeds into a food-processor or blender and purée.

2. Cut chilies in halves and remove seeds. Scald tomatoes in boiling water for 1–2 minutes, remove skins, cut tomatoes up roughly. Place into a large microwave bowl, add chilies. Cook on HIGH until tomatoes are well cooked, about 15–18 minutes. Strain away excess liquid.

3. Add to the tomatoes all other ingredients. Cook on HIGH uncovered until mixture has thickened, about 20–25 minutes.

4. Fill clean jars, cover with a lid. Store pickles 2–3 weeks to mature.

Lime or Lemon Pickles

INGREDIENTS

10 limes or lemons

2 fresh green chilies

2 teaspoons fresh ginger, grated

3 cloves

1 tablespoon mustard seeds

1 teaspoon salt

1 teaspoon black pepper

METHOD

1. Cut unpeeled limes or lemons into thin slices, place in a microwave bowl, sprinkle with salt. Leave to stand over night.
2. Cut chilies in half lengthwise, remove seeds, dice finely, add to limes or lemons along with all other ingredients. Cook on HIGH to heat through, about 2–3 minutes. Cool.
3. Fill clean jar with limes or lemons, cover with a lid. Allow to mature 2–3 weeks before using. The pickles are ready to eat when skins of the fruit are tender.
4. Pickled limes or lemons are served with Indian dishes, curries or papadums.

Mustard Pickles

INGREDIENTS

6–8 onions, small pickling size

2 zucchini

1 red bell pepper

1 small cauliflower

¾ cup flour

1 teaspoon turmeric

10–12 green beans

¾ cup sugar

3 tablespoons dry mustard

2 pints malt vinegar

METHOD

1. Peel onions and leave whole. Slice zucchini into rings and break cauliflower into small pieces. Cut beans in half.
2. Soak vegetables in brine (see page 98) for 24 hours.
3. Mix flour, sugar, mustard, and turmeric with a little vinegar.
4. Cook remaining vinegar on HIGH to boiling point.
5. Stir in blended flour mixture, return to microwave, and cook on HIGH until mixture thickens (about 3–4 minutes).
6. Drain and rinse vegetables, add to thickened sauce and cook on HIGH for 2–3 minutes.
7. Remove vegetables from sauce and pack into clean, warm, sterilized jars.
8. Fill jars to brim with sauce. Cover with lid. Store.

Mixed Vegetable Pickle

INGREDIENTS

1 lb onions

1 cucumber

green or red chilies

1 lb cauliflower

1 lb green beans

1¾ pints spiced vinegar

brine

METHOD

1. Peel onions and cut in half. Cut cucumber into large cubes and break cauliflower into small pieces. Trim and cut beans to 2 inch lengths.
2. Soak vegetables in brine for 24 hours.
3. Drain, rinse in cold water, pack vegetables into clean, warm, sterilized jars.
4. Add a whole chili to each jar.
5. Fill jars to overflowing with spiced vinegar (see page 99).
6. Cover with lid. Store.

Pickled Beet

INGREDIENTS

6 medium-sized beets
1 cup water
1 teaspoon dill seeds
½ pint white vinegar
1 tablespoon mustard seeds
1 cup sugar

METHOD

1. Place beets and water in a microwave-proof bowl.
2. Cook on HIGH until beets are tender and the skin is loose (about 18–20 minutes).
3. Cool, cut off tops and bottoms, pull away skin, and slice.
4. Place remaining ingredients in a microwave-proof bowl and cook until mixture boils. Stir until sugar dissolves.
5. Pack beets into clean, warm, sterilized jars.
6. Fill jars to overflowing with vinegar mixture.
7. Cover with lid, store to mature for 2–3 weeks before using.

Pickled Cherries

INGREDIENTS

1 lb cherries

1 cup water

½ cup dry sherry

1 cup vinegar

½ lb sugar

½ teaspoon allspice

METHOD

1. Remove stems and stones from cherries.
2. Place remaining ingredients in a microwave-proof bowl and cook until mixture boils. Stir until sugar dissolves.
3. Pack cherries into clean, warm, sterilized jars.
4. Fill jars to overflowing with vinegar mixture.
5. Cover with lid. Store.

Pickled Cucumber

INGREDIENTS

4 small unpeeled cucumbers
1¼ cups cider vinegar
2 green bell peppers
½ lb sugar

METHOD

1. Slice cucumbers into thin circles. Cut bell peppers in half, remove seeds and slice into strips.
2. Dissolve sugar in warmed vinegar.
3. Pack vegetables into clean, warm, sterilized jars.
4. Fill jars to overflowing with vinegar mixture.
5. Cover with lid. Store.

Pickled Gherkins

INGREDIENTS
fresh gherkins
spiced vinegar

METHOD
1. Soak gherkins in brine (see page 98) for 3 days.
2. Drain well and dry.
3. Pack gherkins carefully into jars.
4. Bring spiced vinegar to the boil on HIGH.
5. Pour over gherkins till they are covered. Screw on lid and leave for 24 hours.
6. Strain vinegar from gherkins and reheat on HIGH till boiling.
7. Pour over gherkins till they are covered. Screw on lid and leave for another 24 hours.
8. Repeat Steps 6 and 7 until gherkins are a good green color.
9. Before storing, ensure that gherkins are well covered with vinegar.

Pickled Onions

INGREDIENTS
1 lb small pickling onions
1½ pints spiced vinegar
brine

METHOD
1. Peel onions and soak in brine (see page 98) for 24 hours.
2. Drain, rinse in cold water, pack onions into clean, warm, sterilized jars.
3. Fill jars to overflowing with spiced vinegar (see page 99).
4. Cover with lid. Store.

Pickled Red Cabbage

INGREDIENTS

1 lb red cabbage

8 ozs small onions

1½ cups spiced vinegar

½ cup water

¼ cup sugar

¼ cup salt

METHOD

1. Cut cabbage into quarters, remove core, wash well in cold water, drain. Shred cabbage finely, cut shreds into about 1 inch lengths. Cut onion into large dice. Place both vegetables into a glass bowl, sprinkle with salt. Allow to stand for 24 hours, stirring 2–3 times during that period. Drain away excess liquid. Wash cabbage well in clean cold water, drain thoroughly.

2. Heat the vinegar, water, and sugar to boiling point on HIGH, about 1 minute. Stir to dissolve sugar.

3. Pack cabbage into clean jars, cover with hot vinegar. Cover with a lid. Store.

Pickled Walnuts

INGREDIENTS

any quantity of green walnuts

2 pints vinegar

8 whole cloves

2 teaspoons black peppercorns

2–3 bay leaves

2 inches cinnamon stick

1 teaspoon mustard seeds

METHOD

1. Prick walnut shells all over with a sterilized darning needle, place into a glass or ceramic bowl, cover with brine (see page 98) and allow to stand for 8 days. Replace old brine with new and allow to stand a further 14 days.
2. Remove walnuts from brine, wash in cold water. Spread the walnuts onto something flat, exposing them to the air until they turn black.
3. Place walnuts into a jar, cover them with spiced vinegar (see page 99).
4. Cover with a lid. Store 3–4 weeks to mature before using.

Pickled Zucchini

INGREDIENTS

2 lbs zucchini

2 lbs green tomatoes

2 large onions

2 large cucumbers

3 tablespoons salt

3 cups brown vinegar

1 lb sugar

Bouquet garni

Mix together the following in gauze tied up to form a small bag:

½ teaspoon chili powder

¼ teaspoon cayenne pepper

½ teaspoon cloves ground

½ teaspoon whole allspice

½ teaspoon whole black peppercorns

To make paste

Mix together:

2 tablespoons cornflour

1 tablespoon mustard powder

1 dessertspoon turmeric

½ cup water

METHOD

1. Cut all vegetables into small pieces
   (skin can be removed from zucchini or left on.)
2. Place all prepared vegetables in a large glass or plastic bowl.
3. Sprinkle with salt and allow to stand overnight.
4. Next day, drain away excess liquid, add vinegar, sugar, and bouquet
   garni to vegetables and cook on HIGH for 20–40 minutes.
5. While still hot, thicken with prepared paste.
6. Cook a further 3–4 minutes or until mixture is clear.
7. Bottle and seal.
8. Store in a cool, dark cupboard ready for use.

Spicy Red Tomatoes

INGREDIENTS

5 lbs ripe tomatoes

2 lbs brown sugar

3 cups vinegar

1 tablespoon mixed spice

1 tablespoon ground cinnamon

1 teaspoon ground cloves

METHOD

1. Immerse tomatoes in boiling water for 2–3 minutes, then peel off skin.
2. Pack tomatoes into clean, warm sterilized jars.
3. Place sugar, vinegar, and spices in a microwave-proof bowl and cook on HIGH until mixture thickens to the consistency of cream. (about 8–10 minutes).
4. Fill jars to brim with vinegar mixture.
5. Cover with lid. Store.

CHUTNEYS

Chutneys add "bite" to cold meat dishes or sandwiches and can also be stirred into stews or casseroles for added flavor. They can even be added to scrambled eggs or salad dressings for extra flavor. As you'll see from the following recipes, a huge variety of fruits, vegetables, and spices can be used to make a jar of chutney.

Apple Chutney

INGREDIENTS
4 lbs Granny Smith apples
3 medium diced onions
1 lb seeded raisins, chopped
3 lemons
1 tablespoon mustard seeds
3 teaspoons ground ginger
2 lbs brown sugar
3 cups brown vinegar
2 teaspoons salt

METHOD
1. Peel and core apples, dice finely. Place in a microwave-proof bowl with raisins, juice and rind of the lemons, and all other ingredients.
2. Cook uncovered on HIGH until chutney has thickened, about 20–30 minutes.
3. Fill clean jars. Cover with a lid. Store and allow to mature at least 3–4 weeks before using.

Apple and Date Chutney

INGREDIENTS

4 medium cooking apples, peeled, cored, and diced

1 cup chopped, seeded dates

1 teaspoon chili powder

1 cup honey or light molasses

2 cups brown vinegar

¼ teaspoon ground allspice

6 whole cloves

1 tablespoon salt

2 onions

1 cup raisins or sultanas

METHOD

1. Place all ingredients in a large microwave-proof bowl.
2. Cook on HIGH until boiling (about 8–10 minutes).
3. Stir to dissolve sugar.
4. Cook on HIGH for 40–45 minutes or until chutney has thickened.
5. Fill clean, warm jars. Seal with lid while still hot.
6. Store in a cool cupboard for at least 1 week before serving.

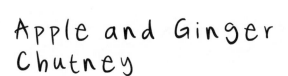

Apple and Ginger Chutney

INGREDIENTS
2 lbs cooking apples

3 ozs green ginger

1 cup white vinegar

1½ cups brown sugar

½ teaspoon ground allspice

½ teaspoon salt

1 medium onion

1 bell pepper

½ cup sultanas

1 tablespoon lemon rind

METHOD
1. Peel, core and dice apples, onions, and bell pepper.
2. Peel ginger and crush or chop finely.
3. Place all ingredients in a microwave-proof bowl.
4. Cook on HIGH until boiling, about 6–8 minutes.
5. Stir to dissolve sugar.
6. Continue cooking on HIGH until chutney has thickened, about 15–20 minutes.
7. Fill clean, warm jars. Seal with lid while still hot. Store in a cool cupboard.

Bell Pepper Chutney

INGREDIENTS

6 red bell peppers

6 green bell peppers

2 large onions

1½ cups vinegar

½ lb sugar

1 teaspoon salt

1 cup water

METHOD

1. Remove stems, veins, and seeds from bell peppers. Peel onions. Roughly chop bell peppers and onions and place in a microwave-proof bowl.
2. Add water and cook on HIGH for about 6–8 minutes, until tender.
3. Drain off excess water.
4. Blend or mash vegetables together and add all other ingredients.
5. Cover and cook on HIGH until boiling. Stir to dissolve sugar fully.
6. Return mixture to microwave and cook uncovered on HIGH for about 15–20 minutes, until mixture has thickened.
7. Fill clean, warm, sterilized jars to the brim.
8. Label and date jars.

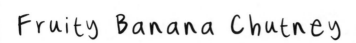

Fruity Banana Chutney

INGREDIENTS

12 bananas

¾ cup dates, halved and stoned

½ cup raisins

1 cup sugar

1 dessertspoon cinnamon

2 cups malt vinegar

½ cup sultanas

1 dessertspoon salt

1 teaspoon nutmeg

2 teaspoon turmeric

METHOD

1. Peel and slice bananas.
2. Place all ingredients in a microwave-proof bowl and cook on HIGH until mixture thickens (about 15–20 minutes). Stir 2–3 times during cooking.
3. Pack chutney into clean, warm, sterilized jars. Cover with lid. Store.

Green Tomato Chutney

INGREDIENTS

1 lb green tomatoes

1 large cooking apple

1 clove crushed garlic

½ cup sugar

1 teaspoon ground ginger

2 medium onions

1 green bell pepper

3 green chilies

½ cup malt vinegar

½ teaspoon salt

METHOD

1. Coarsely chop tomatoes, onions, and apples. Dice bell pepper, removing stem, seeds and white pith. Slit open chilies, remove seeds and chop finely.
2. Place all ingredients in a microwave-proof bowl, cover with a loose-fitting lid, or pierced plastic wrap (steam needs to escape during cooking), and cook on HIGH until mixture thickens (approximately 15–20 minutes).
3. Pack chutney into clean, warm, sterilized jars. Cover with lid. Store.

Mango Chutney

INGREDIENTS
4 medium-sized mangoes
3 cooking apples
¾ lb onions
1 lb brown sugar
2 cups brown vinegar
1 cup water
1 dessertspoon ground ginger
1 teaspoon allspice
1 teaspoon salt

METHOD
1. Peel mangoes, cut pieces away from stone. Peel, core, and roughly chop apple. Peel and dice onions.
2. Place mango, apple, onion pieces, and water in a microwave-proof bowl. Cook on HIGH until tender (about 20–25 minutes).
3. Add sugar and stir until dissolved.
4. Stir in remaining ingredients and cook on HIGH until mixture thickens (about 20–25 minutes).
5. Pack chutney into clean, warm, sterilized jars. Cover with lid. Store.

Mushroom and Chayote Chutney

INGREDIENTS

1 lb mushrooms

4 chayote

2 Granny Smith apples

1 bell pepper, red or green

½ cup spiced vinegar

1 cup sugar

METHOD

1. Peel mushrooms and remove stalks. Slice thinly. Peel, core, and finely dice apples and chayote. Remove stem, veins, and seeds from bell pepper, and dice finely.
2. Place all ingredients in a large microwave-proof bowl.
3. Cover and cook on HIGH for about 2–3 minutes, until boiling. Stir to dissolve sugar fully.
4. Return mixture to microwave and cook uncovered on HIGH for approximately 25–35 minutes, until fruit is tender and mixture has thickened.
5. Fill clean, warm, sterilized jars to the brim.
6. Vacuum seal according to directions on page 71.
7. Label and date jars.

Pawpaw Chutney

INGREDIENTS

4 lbs pawpaw
6 cloves crushed garlic
3 red chilies
3 ozs freshly grated ginger
1½ pints spiced vinegar
1¼ lbs sugar
1 teaspoon salt

METHOD

1. Peel pawpaw, cut in half, remove and discard seeds. Cut fruit into small cubes. Place into a large microwave-proof bowl. Add all other ingredients.
2. Cook on HIGH to boiling point, about 8–10 minutes. Stir to dissolve sugar.
3. Continue cooking on HIGH uncovered until chutney has thickened, about 15–20 minutes.
4. Fill clean jars, cover with lid. Store.

Peach Chutney

INGREDIENTS

4 lbs yellow cooking peaches

1 lb brown sugar

½ teaspoon cayenne pepper

2 pints vinegar

3 ozs green ginger

1 tablespoon crushed garlic

1 cup raisins

METHOD

1. Peel peaches with a stainless steel knife or a peeling utensil, or immerse in boiling water for 2 minutes then pull away skin.
2. Slice peaches and place in a microwave-proof bowl. Cook on HIGH for 8–10 minutes.
3. Add sugar and stir until dissolved.
4. Reheat on HIGH until mixture is consistency of a preserve (about 15–18 minutes) and cool.
5. Chop ginger and raisins finely.
6. Add all ingredients to peaches and cook on HIGH for 8–10 minutes.
7. Pack chutney into clean, warm, sterilized jars. Cover with lid. Store.

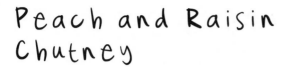

Peach and Raisin Chutney

INGREDIENTS

2 lbs yellow-fleshed peaches

4 Granny Smith apples

2 cups raisins

2 cups chopped celery

1 bell pepper, red or green

2 cups vinegar

1 lb sugar

METHOD

1. Peel and stone peaches, and chop roughly. Peel, core, and dice apples. Remove stem, veins, and seeds from bell pepper and dice.
2. Place all ingredients in a large microwave-proof bowl.
3. Cover and cook on HIGH until boiling. Stir to dissolve sugar fully.
4. Return mixture to microwave and cook uncovered on HIGH for about 20–25 minutes, until fruit is tender and mixture has thickened.
5. Fill clean, warm, sterilized jars to the brim.
6. Vacuum seal according to directions on page 71.
7. Label and date jars.

Plum Chutney

INGREDIENTS

2 lbs dark red or blue plums

1½ lbs cooking apples

1 cup brown vinegar

1 teaspoon salt

½ lb onions

½ lb brown sugar

½ cup water

1 teaspoon whole cloves

1 teaspoon black peppercorns

1 teaspoon allspice

METHOD

1. Wash plums, halve and remove stone. Peel and core apples, then chop roughly. Peel and dice onions.
2. Place in a microwave-proof bowl with water and cook on HIGH until tender (about 8–10 minutes).
3. Tie spices in a muslin bag and place in a microwave-proof bowl with sugar and vinegar. Cook on HIGH until liquid boils.
4. Stir until sugar dissolves.
5. Reheat on HIGH and boil for 2–3 minutes. Remove muslin bag.
6. Pour vinegar into fruit and vegetable mixture.
7. Cook on HIGH until mixture thickens (about 15–18 minutes).
8. Pack chutney into clean, warm, sterilized jars. Cover with lid. Store.

Red Tomato Chutney

INGREDIENTS

2 lbs ripe tomatoes

2 large cooking apples

½ lb onions

½ cup sultanas

½ cup raisins

½ lb brown sugar

1 cup vinegar

1 teaspoon prepared mustard

1 teaspoon ground allspice

1 teaspoon salt

METHOD

1. Immerse tomatoes in boiling water for 2–3 minutes, peel off skin.
2. Roughly cut up tomatoes and onions. Peel, core, and dice apples.
3. Place all ingredients in a large microwave-proof bowl.
4. Cook on HIGH until boiling, approximately 6–8 minutes.
5. Stir to dissolve sugar.
6. Continue cooking on HIGH until chutney has thickened, approximately 18–20 minutes.
7. Fill clean, warm jars. Seal with lid while still hot.

Tamarillo Chutney

INGREDIENTS

30 tamarillos

4 cooking apples

3 onions, diced

2 cups dates, chopped

1 oz fresh ginger, grated

2 cups brown vinegar

4½ cups brown sugar

2 teaspoon mixed spices

1 teaspoon cayenne pepper

2 teaspoons salt

METHOD

1. Scald tamarillos in boiling water 1-2 minutes, remove skins. Roughly cut up tamarillos.
2. Peel and core apples, cut into small dice. Scrape skin from ginger before grating.
3. Place all ingredients into a large microwave-proof bowl. Cook uncovered on HIGH, 10–15 minutes. Stir to dissolve sugar.
4. Continue cooking on HIGH until mixture has thickened, about 30–40 minutes.
5. Fill clean jars, cover with a lid. Store.

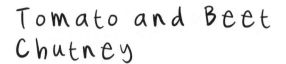

Tomato and Beet Chutney

INGREDIENTS

2 lbs tomatoes

2 lbs beets

2 large onions, diced

3 cups vinegar

1½ cups sugar

½ teaspoon cayenne pepper

2 teaspoons turmeric

2 tablespoons all-purpose flour

2 teaspoons salt

METHOD

1. Place beets in a large microwave-proof bowl, cover with water. Cook on HIGH until tender and skins are easily removed, approx 20–30 minutes. (The cooking time is determined by the size and age of the beets). Cool. Remove skins with your fingers, discard. The skin will come away very easily. Coarsely grate or mince beet.
2. Cut up unpeeled tomatoes into large pieces. Place into a large microwave-proof bowl, add onions. Cook on HIGH uncovered about 15–20 minutes or until tender.
3. Blend flour with a little water to form a thin paste, stir into the tomatoes, add all other ingredients. Cook uncovered on HIGH a further 20–30 minutes or until chutney has thickened.
4. Fill clean jars, cover with lid. Store.

Tomato and Chayote Chutney

INGREDIENTS

4 large chayote

¾ cup currants

3 cups vinegar

2 cups sugar

6 whole cloves

3 onions, diced

¼ teaspoon cayenne pepper

2 lbs ripe tomatoes

½ teaspoon salt

METHOD

1. Scald tomatoes in boiling water for 1–2 minutes, remove skins. Peel and core chayote. Roughly chop up both.
2. Place all ingredients in a large microwave-proof bowl. Cook on HIGH to boiling point, stir to dissolve sugar. Continue cooking uncovered until chutney has thickened, about 30–40 minutes.
3. Fill clean jars, cover with a lid. Store.

Tomato and Pumpkin Chutney

INGREDIENTS
1 lb ripe tomatoes
2 lbs pumpkin (dry)
2 large onions, diced
1 clove garlic, crushed
1 cup raisins, chopped
1½ cups vinegar
1 lb brown sugar
1½ teaspoons mixed spice
1 level tablespoon salt

METHOD
1. Scald tomatoes in boiling water for 1–2 minutes, remove skins. Cut tomatoes up roughly, place in a large microwave-proof bowl.
2. Peel and remove seeds from the pumpkin, cut into small pieces. Add to tomatoes along with all other ingredients.
3. Cook uncovered on HIGH until chutney has thickened, about 25–35 minutes. Stir once or twice during that time.
4. Fill clean jars, cover with lid. Store.

Note: The cooking time is determined by the dryness of the pumpkin. The drier the pumpkin the shorter the cooking time.

RELISHES

Try these versatile relishes. They're easy to make, and great for enlivening cold collations in summer.

Hot Chayote Relish

INGREDIENTS

4 chayote

3 medium onions

3 large cooking apples

½ cup sultanas

½ cup raisins

1½ cups brown sugar

2 cups vinegar

2 teaspoons of turmeric

2 teaspoons prepared mustard

1 teaspoon each of cayenne pepper, curry powder, salt

1 clove crushed garlic

METHOD

1. Peel chayote, onions, and apples, remove and discard cores.
2. Dice finely and place in a large microwave-proof bowl, add all other ingredients. Cook on HIGH until boiling point, about 2–3 minutes. Stir to dissolve sugar. Continue cooking on high 30–35 minutes or until relish has thickened.
3. Fill clean jars with hot relish. Seal with a lid. Cool and store.

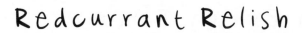

Redcurrant Relish

INGREDIENTS

4 lbs redcurrants

1 lb onions

½ lb brown sugar

1½ cups brown vinegar

1 oz green ginger

3 cloves garlic

1 teaspoon turmeric

1 teaspoon cardamom

1 teaspoon salt

METHOD

1. Cut tops of currants, dice onions, scrape and discard skin from ginger, grate finely, crush garlic.
2. Place all ingredients into a large microwave-proof bowl. Cook uncovered on HIGH until relish has thickened, about 25–35 minutes.
3. Fill clean jars, cover with lid. Store.

Rich and Fruity Tomato Relish

INGREDIENTS

2 lbs ripe tomatoes

1 lb cooking apples

1 lemon

½ cup orange juice

½ cup brown vinegar

1 cup seeded raisins

½ cup brown sugar

½ teaspoon allspice

salt to taste

METHOD

1. Scald tomatoes in boiling water, 1–2 minutes, remove skins, cut tomatoes into large chunks.
2. Peel and core apples, cut into large pieces. Slice unpeeled lemon thinly, then into quarters.
3. Place all ingredients into a large microwave-proof bowl. Cook on HIGH until mixture has thickened, about 25–30 minutes.
4. Fill clean jars, cover with a lid.

Spotty Red Bell Pepper Relish

INGREDIENTS

2 lbs ripe tomatoes

3 lbs red bell pepper

3 medium white onions

1 cup sugar

½ cup currants

2 cups white vinegar

2 cloves garlic

salt to taste

METHOD

1. Scald tomatoes in boiling water 1–2 minutes. Peel away skins. Chop tomatoes up roughly. Cut bell pepper in half remove seeds and pith. Dice onions and bell pepper finely. Place into a microwave-proof bowl and cook on HIGH 6–8 minutes.
2. Add remaining ingredients and cook uncovered on HIGH until mixture has thickened, about 30–40 minutes.
3. Fill clean jars, cover with a lid.

Spicy Rhubarb Relish

INGREDIENTS

2 lbs rhubarb
1¼ lbs sugar
1 cup raisins
1 teaspoon ground cinnamon
1 teaspoon ground mixed spice
½ teaspoon ground nutmeg
½ teaspoon ground cloves
1 cup brown vinegar

METHOD

1. Trim base and leaves from rhubarb. Cut stalks into 1-inch lengths. Cut raisins in half.
2. Place all ingredients into a large microwave-proof bowl. Cook on HIGH 10–12 minutes, stir to dissolve sugar. Continue cooking on HIGH until mixture has thickened, about 25–30 minutes.
3. Fill clean jars, cover with a lid.

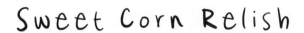

Sweet Corn Relish

INGREDIENTS

¾ lb sweet corn kernels

1 red and 1 green bell pepper

1 chopped onion

1½ cups white vinegar

⅓ cup sugar

2 teaspoons turmeric

1 tablespoon prepared mustard

1 teaspoon ground black pepper

1 clove garlic, crushed

1 tablespoon vegetable oil

1 tablespoon cornflour

METHOD

1. Remove and discard core seeds and pith from bell peppers. Finely dice bell peppers. Place in a large microwave-proof bowl along with all other ingredients, except for cornflour.
2. Cook on HIGH 3–4 minutes or until onion has cleared. Blend cornflour in 3 tablespoons water, stir into hot relish. Return to microwave, cook on HIGH to boiling point and boil for 1 minute.
3. Fill clean jars. Seal and store.

Tropical Fruit Relish

INGREDIENTS

1 lb preserved pineapple

3–4 mangoes

2 onions

2 green chilies

2 red chilies

1 oz root ginger

1 cup vinegar

1½ cups sugar

1 teaspoon salt

1 teaspoon nutmeg

METHOD

1. Cut chilies in half lengthwise, remove seeds. Peel mangoes, remove and discard stones, finely dice mangoes. Scrape and discard skin from ginger. Finely chop or process ginger, onion, chilies, and pineapple.

2. Place all ingredients into a microwave-proof bowl. Cook on HIGH until mixture has thickened, about 25–35 minutes. Fill clean jars, cover with lid. Store.

6

Sugarless Fruit Spreads and Chutneys

With the combination of microwave cooking and artificial sweeteners, it is now possible to produce a sugarless, jelly-like spread. The spreads included here are simply fruit pulp to which an artificial sweetener is added when opened for use. (If artificial sweetener is cooked with the fruit it can result in a bitter aftertaste.) The sweetener can be added to the fruit just before canning or on serving. The latter is better, as you can adjust it to taste.

Rather than trying to make large quantities of spreads when fresh fruit is available, you may find it easier to make smaller quantities of spreads from your sugarless "Just Fruit" preserves throughout the year. This will give you greater variety.

Also included here are two sugarless chutneys.

Note: These spreads must be vacuum sealed for long-keeping because without the assistance of sugar they will ferment within a few days. Use small jars so that the contents can be used up quickly after the seal is broken. Once opened, store the spreads in the refrigerator for up to one week.

SUGARLESS FRUIT SPREADS

METHOD

1. Choose firm, unblemished fruit. Any bruising should be cut away and discarded.
2. Wash the fruit and peel it if necessary. Halve, and remove any pips or stones.
3. Place fruit in a large microwave-proof bowl.
4. Cook on HIGH until fruit is soft and pulpy.
5. Break up fruit with fork or potato-masher or blender.
6. Return to oven (uncovered) and cook on HIGH until fruit is of a thick jelly-like consistency.
7. Fill clean, sterilized jars to the brim.
8. Fit screw-on lid with sealing ring.
9. Vacuum seal by cooking on MEDIUM HIGH for one minute, adding 30 seconds for each additional jar.
10. Store in a cool, dark cupboard.
11. On opening, add artificial sweetener to taste.

BASIC FRUIT SPREADS

Ingredients and Cooking Times

SPREAD	INGREDIENTS	COOKING TIME (Approx. in minutes)
Apple and raspberry	*3 cooking apples* *3 cups fresh raspberries*	16–18
Apricot	*24 apricots*	14–16
Blackberry	*1 lb blackberries*	12–16
Blackberry and plum	*2 cups blackberries* *8–10 blood plums*	16–18
Banana and apple	*1 banana* *1 cooking apple* *juice of ½ lemon*	5–8
Cherry and cantaloupe	*1 lb cherries* *½ lb cantaloupe* *juice of ½ lemon*	15–18
Mango and banana	*1 mango* *1 banana* *juice of ½ lemon*	6–8
Plum	*2 lbs cherry damson or blood plums*	20–24
Plum and apple	*1 lb plums* *1 lb cooking apples*	18–20

SUGARLESS CHUTNEYS

Sugarless Plum Chutney Spread

INGREDIENTS

1 lb dark red or blue plums

2 medium cooking apples

½ cup brown vinegar

1 large onion

½ teaspoon allspice

3 whole cloves

METHOD

1. Wash plums and remove stones. Peel and core apples and chop roughly.
2. Dice onions and combine with plums, apples, and vinegar.
3. Cook on HIGH in a microwave-proof bowl until tender, about 6–8 minutes.
4. Add allspice and cloves, boil on HIGH for another 3–4 minutes or until chutney has thickened.
5. Remove cloves if desired.
6. Fill clean, sterilized jars to the brim. Fit screw-on lids with sealing ring.
7. Vacuum seal by cooking on MEDIUM HIGH for 1 minute, adding 30 seconds for each additional jar.
8. Store in a cool, dark cupboard.
9. On opening, add artificial sweetener to taste.

Sugarless Red Tomato Chutney Spread

INGREDIENTS

1 lb tomatoes

1 medium apple, peeled, and cored

1 medium peeled onion

1 small green bell pepper

1 clove crushed garlic

¼ cup vinegar

½ teaspoon ground ginger

½ teaspoon salt

METHOD

1. Coarsely chop tomatoes and dice onion, apple and bell pepper, discarding peel, core, and seeds.
2. Place all ingredients in a microwave-proof bowl and leave uncovered.
3. Cook on HIGH until mixture has thickened, about 10–12 minutes.
4. Fill clean, sterilized jars to the brim. Fit screw-on lids with sealing ring.
5. Vacuum seal by cooking on MEDIUM-HIGH for one minute, adding 30 seconds for each additional jar.
6 Store in a cook, dark cupboard.
7. On opening, add artificial sweetener to taste.

7

Fruit and Nut Spreads

Fruit butters make a welcome change from the usual preserves, and are especially popular with sweet-toothed children. Once sealed in the jar, these butters will keep for several weeks in a cool, dark cupboard.

Apple Butter

INGREDIENTS

2 lbs cooking apples
1 cup water
2 tablespoons lemon juice
½ cup sugar
1 dessertspoon cinnamon
¼ teaspoon ground cloves

METHOD

1. Place washed, roughly cut-up apples (retaining skins and cores) in a microwave-proof bowl. Add water and lemon juice.
2. Cook on HIGH for about 8–10 minutes or until apples are soft.
3. Purée in a food-processor or blender.
4. Return apples to a microwave-proof bowl and add sugar and spices.
5. Cook on HIGH for approximately 6–8 minutes or until mixture has thickened and holds its shape when tested on a cold plate.
6. Fill clean, sterilized jars. Secure lids.
7. Vacuum seal as directed on page 71.

Apricot Butter

INGREDIENTS

2 lbs apricots

½ cup sugar

½ cup water

pinch nutmeg

½ teaspoon cinnamon

METHOD

1. Halve apricots and remove stones. Add water.
2. Cook on HIGH for about 8–10 minutes or until apricots are soft.
3. Purée in a food-processor or blender.
4. Return apricots to a microwave-proof bowl and add sugar and spices.
5. Cook on HIGH for approximately 6–8 minutes or until mixture has thickened and holds its shape when tested on a cold plate.
6. Fill clean, sterilized jars. Secure lids.
7. Vacuum seal as directed on page 71.

Crunchy Peanut Butter

INGREDIENTS
1 lb unsalted roasted peanuts
½ teaspoon salt
¼–½ cup cooking oil

METHOD
1. Remove husks, if any, by spreading peanuts evenly over carousel plate. Cook on HIGH for 2–3 minutes or until husks rub off easily. Discard.
2. Crush half the peanuts in a food-processor until they are small pieces. Remove.
3. Blend the remaining peanuts with oil to a smooth paste, then add the crushed peanuts and blend until just mixed.
4. Fill clean, sterilized jars to ½ inch from lip.
5. Release any air from jar by sliding a knife or packing stick into air pockets.
6. Fit screw-on lids with built-in seals.
7. Cook as follows:

JAR SIZE	OVEN SETTING	COOKING TIME
8 ounces	medium high	2 minutes
16 ounces	medium high	3 minutes
28 ounces	medium high	4 minutes

Note: Settings assume one jar in a 650-watt oven. If varying power or number of jars, adjust settings using tables on page 9.

8. Cool and store in a dark cupboard.

Lemon Butter

INGREDIENTS
rind and juice of 2 lemons
2 ozs butter
4 ozs sugar
2 large eggs, beaten

METHOD
1. Mix all ingredients in a microwave-proof bowl.
2. Cook on MEDIUM HIGH for 6–8 minutes or until butter has thickened, stirring once to dissolve sugar during this cooking time.
3. Fill clean, sterilized jars. Secure lids.
4. Vacuum seal as directed on page 71.

Orange Butter

INGREDIENTS
rind and juice of 2 oranges
2 ozs butter
4 ozs sugar
2 large eggs, beaten

METHOD
1. Mix all ingredients in a microwave-proof bowl.
2. Cook on MEDIUM HIGH for 6–8 minutes or until butter has thickened.
3. Fill clean, sterilized jars. Secure lids.
4. Vacuum seal as directed on page 71.

Passionfruit Butter

INGREDIENTS

pulp of 8 passionfruit

2 ozs butter

4 ozs sugar

2 large eggs, beaten

METHOD

1. Mix all ingredients in a microwave-proof bowl.
2. Cook on MEDIUM HIGH for 6–8 minutes or until butter has thickened.
3. Fill clean, sterilized jars. Secure lids.
4. Vacuum seal as directed on page 71.

8

Savory Sauces and Salsas

So many dishes can be transformed or greatly enhanced by the right sauce. Some sauces are made with the meal and served immediately. Others can be bottled and stored ready for future occasions. All recipes given here use considerably less than the traditional amount of sugar.

Vacuum Sealing Sauces

If directed by the recipe, vacuum seal according to instructions for preserves (page 71), but use the cooking times below. These apply to one jar only. For every additional jar add 1 minute's extra cooking time.

JAR SIZE	OVEN SETTING	COOKING TIME
8 ounces	medium high	2 minutes
16 ounces	medium high	3 minutes
28 ounces	medium high	4 minutes

Apple Sauce

INGREDIENTS

3–4 cooking apples

1 oz butter

1 cup water

squeeze of lemon juice

sugar to taste

METHOD

1. Peel, core, and dice apples.
2. Cook apples and water in a heat resistant microwave-proof bowl on HIGH until tender, about 6–10 minutes.
3. Mash apples to a purée with a fork or in a blender.
4. Before serving, stir in butter, lemon juice, and sugar to taste.
5. Can be stored in airtight jar in the refrigerator for 1–2 weeks. Serve with roast pork.

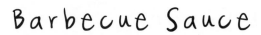

Barbecue Sauce

INGREDIENTS
2 cups ketchup
⅓ cup Worcestershire sauce
⅓ cup brown vinegar
1 tablespoon crushed garlic
1 teaspoon prepared mustard

METHOD
1. Place all ingredients in a microwave-proof bowl and stir together.
2. Cook on HIGH for 2–3 minutes.
3. Fill clean sauce bottles, seal, and store.

Cumberland Sauce

INGREDIENTS

1 orange

1 lemon

4 tablespoons sugar

4 tablespoons port wine

2 teaspoons cornflour, blended with
  2 teaspoons water

METHOD

1. Peel the rind thinly from the orange and lemon and cut into fine strips.
2. Place in a microwave-proof bowl and cover with ½ cup water. Cook on HIGH for 3–4 minutes. Set aside.
3. Squeeze juice from both fruits and heat on HIGH for 30–60 seconds.
4. Quickly stir in sugar to dissolve. Cook on HIGH for a further 2–3 minutes.
5. Add port, blended cornflour. Cook to thicken.
6. Drain water from cooked rind and stir into sauce.
7. While still hot, fill clean, sterilized jars, fit lids. Store.
8. Vacuum seal for longer storage life (see page 71).

Note: If sauce has been allowed to cool, add 1 minute to specified sealing times.

9. Label and date jars. Serve with ham or lamb.

Curry Sauce

INGREDIENTS

2 cooking apples

2 medium onions

3 tablespoons curry powder

2 oz all-purpose flour

4 cups water or beef stock

3 tablespoons sweet chutney

2 tablespoons tomato paste

2 tablespoons cooking oil

juice of ½ lemon

METHOD

1. Peel, core, and dice apples.
2. Stir curry powder into ½ cup of stock and allow to stand at least 10 minutes. This is for added flavor.
3. Blend flour into curry mixture.
4. Place all ingredients into a large covered, microwave-proof bowl and cook on MEDIUM HIGH for 20–25 minutes.
5. While still hot, fill clean, sterilized jars. Fit lids, store.

Haricot Beans in Tomato Sauce

INGREDIENTS

¾ lb haricot beans

2 tablespoons tomato paste

1 bay leaf

salt to taste

1 teaspoon onion powder

½ teaspoon thyme

2 teaspoons sugar

METHOD

1. Cover beans with water, heat to boiling point on HIGH, and allow to stand over night, strain away water.
2. Add all other ingredients except tomato paste to the beans, cover with water by 1–2 inches, cover with lid.
3. Cook on MEDIUM HIGH 20–30 minutes or until beans are tender. Cool. Strain water from beans and reserve, remove bay leaf.
4. Place about half the beans into a food-processor, blend to purée and return to remaining beans. Stir in tomato paste and a little cooking liquid if necessary to make a creamy sauce.
5. Fill clean recycled jars with the bean mixture, cover with a metal lid.
6. Preserve and vacuum seal as per chart below.

JAR SIZE	OVEN SETTING	COOKING TIME
8 ounces	medium high	2 minutes
16 ounces	medium high	3 minutes
28 ounces	medium high	4 minutes

Note: Cooking times are for 1 jar.

Check the power of your microwave and adjust the setting if necessary (see page 9).

Horseradish Sauce

INGREDIENTS

½ cup grated horseradish root

1 tablespoon vinegar

2 tablespoons sugar

1 tablespoon cream

1 cup plain yogurt

METHOD

1. Place horseradish, vinegar, and sugar in a microwave-proof bowl and heat on HIGH for 30–60 seconds.
2. Stir to dissolve sugar. Allow to cool.
3. Stir in cream and yogurt.
4. Allow to stand 2–3 hours before serving with beef, or keep in an airtight jar in the refrigerator for up to 2 weeks.

Mild Herb and Tomato Salsa

INGREDIENTS

2 lbs tomatoes

¼ cup diced onions

½ cup bell pepper

1 teaspoon ground coriander

1 teaspoon ground cumin

1 teaspoon chopped parsley

½ cup lemon or lime juice

salt and pepper to taste

METHOD

1. Scald tomatoes in boiling water for 1–2 minutes. Remove skins. Cut tomatoes in half and squeeze out and discard seeds. Cut remaining tomatoes into small pieces. Place into a microwave-proof bowl.
2. Peel and dice onion, cut bell pepper in half and remove and discard seeds and any pith. Chop bell pepper into small dices. Add to tomato along with all other ingredients.
3. Cook uncovered on HIGH until tomatoes and vegetables are tender and mixture has thickened, about 15–20 minutes.
4. Fill clean jars with hot salsa, cover with a metal lid. Cool and store.

Mixed Herb Sauce

INGREDIENTS

½ cup diced onion

½ cup cream

¼ cup dry white wine

¼ cup white vinegar

6 ozs softened butter

1 teaspoon chopped dill

1 teaspoon chopped tarragon

1 teaspoon chopped parsley

METHOD

1. Place diced onions in a microwave-proof bowl, cover, cook on HIGH for 2–3 minutes, add vinegar and wine, cook for a further 2–3 minutes.
2. Add butter, a little at a time, cool slightly. Stir in cream and herbs.
3. Serve warm with steamed vegetables.
4. For keeping, store in refrigerator for up to one week.

No-Tears Tomato Sauce

INGREDIENTS

4 lbs ripe tomatoes

1 cooking apple

1 tablespoon crushed garlic

¾ lb sugar

1 oz salt

¾ cup spiced vinegar (see page 99)

METHOD

1. Roughly chop tomatoes and apple.
2. Cook in a large microwave-proof bowl until tender, about 20–25 minutes.
3. Pour away about half the tomato liquid. (This can be used in soups, casseroles, etc.)
4. Purée tomatoes and apple in a food-processor or blender, strain of skins and seeds and return to bowl.
5. Stir in sugar, salt, and spiced vinegar.
6. Heat to boiling point on HIGH. Stir to dissolve sugar. Continue boiling until sauce has thickened, about 20–30 minutes. Stir 2–3 times during this cooking period.
7. Allow to cool for about 10 minutes.
8. Fill clean, warm, sterilized jars or bottles, seal with lid and store in a cool cupboard.

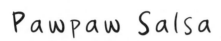

Pawpaw Salsa

INGREDIENTS

2 cups pawpaw

½ cup diced onions

1–2 red chilies

1 teaspoon crushed garlic

½ cup lemon or lime juice

2 tablespoons olive oil

salt and pepper to taste

METHOD

1. Peel pawpaw, cut in half, and remove and discard seeds. Cut pawpaw into small pieces and place into a microwave-proof bowl.
2. Cook diced onion covered in a small microwave-proof bowl for 2–4 minutes or until tender. Cool and add to pawpaw.
3. Cut chilies in half lengthwise, discard seeds. Finely dice chilies and add to pawpaw along with all other ingredients. Cover and allow to stand for at least 1 hour.
4. Drain away excessive liquids. Cook uncovered on HIGH for 3–5 minutes.
5. Fill clean jars with hot salsa, cover with a metal lid. Cool and store.

Pesto

INGREDIENTS

1 cup pine nuts	*12 fresh basil leaves*
¾ cup olive oil	*4 cloves garlic*
salt and pepper to taste	*¼ cup Parmesan cheese*

METHOD

1. Place pine nuts into a small microwave-proof bowl.
2. Thoroughly mix through pine nuts and 1 teaspoon of the oil to coat. Cook on HIGH until golden-brown, about 1–3 minutes. Drain on absorbent paper.
3. Place basil leaves, garlic, and pine nuts into a food-processor, blend to a smooth paste. With processor on slow, gradually add oil. Add salt and pepper to taste, process a further 2–4 seconds.
4. Preserve and vacuum seal as per chart below.

JAR SIZE	OVEN SETTING	COOKING TIME
8 ounces	medium high	2 minutes
16 ounces	medium high	3 minutes
28 ounces	medium high	5 minutes

Note: Cooking times are for 1 jar. Add 1 minute for every additional jar.

Check the power of your microwave and adjust the setting if necessary (see page 9).

To Serve Pesto: Remove pesto from jar, stir through grated Parmesan. Add to hot freshly cooked pasta. Reheat if necessary on HIGH 2–3 minutes. Top with a little more Parmesan.

Pineapple Salsa

INGREDIENTS

3 cups crushed pineapple

¼ cup sugar

½ cup diced onion

½ cup green bell pepper

1 teaspoon fresh ginger

1 teaspoon mustard powder

METHOD

1. Remove and discard seeds and any pith from bell pepper.
   Finely chop. Scrape and discard skin from ginger. Grate ginger.
2. Place all ingredients into a microwave-proof bowl. Cook on
   HIGH for 10–12 minutes or until salsa has thickened slightly.
3. Fill clean jars with hot salsa, cover with a metal lid.
   Cool and store.

Pizza Base Sauce

INGREDIENTS

4 lbs tomatoes

2 tablespoons sugar

2 teaspoons freshly chopped oregano

2 teaspoons freshly chopped basil

2 cloves garlic

salt to taste

METHOD

1. Scald tomatoes in boiling water for 2–3 minutes, peel away skins and discard. Roughly cut up tomatoes, place into microwave-proof bowl. Add all other ingredients.
2. Cook uncovered on HIGH until tomatoes are soft, about 15–20 minutes. Pour away excessive liquid, cook for a further 5–10 minutes and cool.
3. Place mixture into a blender or a Mouli and purée.
4. Fill clean sterilized jars, cover with a metal lid.
5. Preserve and vacuum seal as per chart below.

JAR SIZE	OVEN SETTING	COOKING TIME
8 ounces	medium high	2 minutes
16 ounces	medium high	3 minutes
28 ounces	medium high	4 minutes

Note: Cooking times are for 1 jar. Add 2 minutes for every additional jar.

Check the power of your microwave and adjust the setting if necessary (see page 9).

Pizzaiola

INGREDIENTS

3 cups bottled tomatoes

2 teaspoons crushed garlic

½ teaspoon marjoram

2 teaspoons dried parsley

salt and pepper to taste

METHOD

1. Place tomatoes and half the liquid into a food-processor, blend to a purée. Transfer to a microwave-proof bowl, add marjoram and garlic, season with salt and pepper.
2. Cook uncovered on HIGH for 12–15 minutes or until sauce is reduced to half. Stir in parsley.
3. Fill clean recycled jars, fit with a metal lid which has a built-in sealing ring.
4. Preserve and vacuum seal according to the chart below.

JAR SIZE	OVEN SETTING	COOKING TIME
8 ounces	medium high	2 minutes
16 ounces	medium high	3 minutes
28 ounces	medium high	5 minutes

Note: Cooking times are for 1 jar. Add 1 minute for every additional jar.

Check the power of your microwave and adjust the setting if necessary (see page 9).

Plum Sauce

INGREDIENTS

4½ lbs blood plums

16 oz sugar

2 teaspoons salt

1 teaspoon allspice and cloves

2 cups vinegar

½ tablespoon cayenne pepper

1 small piece fresh ginger, bruised

METHOD

1. Wash plums well and remove stems, cut up roughly. Place all ingredients into a large (about one gallon) microwave-proof bowl.
2. Cook on HIGH 20–25 minutes or until fruit is very soft, and sauce has thickened. Cool. Remove stones.
3. Purée in a food-processor or blender, strain to remove skins.
4. Fill clean sauce bottles, seal and store.

Red Hot Tomato Salsa

INGREDIENTS

2 lbs tomatoes

½ cup diced onions

2 cloves crushed garlic

2 red chilies

2 tablespoons fresh coriander

3 tablespoons white vinegar

2 tablespoons olive oil

salt and ground pepper to taste

METHOD

1. Scald tomatoes in boiling water for 1–2 minutes. Remove skins.
2. Cut tomatoes in half and squeeze out seeds and discard.
   Cut tomatoes into small pieces. Place into a microwave-proof bowl.
3. Peel and dice onion, cut chilies in half lengthwise and discard seeds.
   Chop chilies into small dice, crush garlic and add to tomatoes.
4. Cook on HIGH uncovered until tomatoes are tender, about
   12–15 minutes. Add all other ingredients and boil a further
   5–10 minutes, or until salsa has thickened slightly.
5. Fill clean recycled jars with hot salsa, fit with metal lid. Cool and
   store.

Spaghetti in Tomato Sauce

INGREDIENTS

2 lbs ripe tomatoes

1 tablespoon sugar

salt and pepper to taste

2 medium onions, diced

2 teaspoons fresh basil, chopped

¾ lb spaghetti

METHOD

1. Scald tomatoes in boiling water for 1–2 minutes. Remove skins. Roughly cut up tomatoes.
1. Place tomatoes and onions into a microwave-proof bowl. Cook on HIGH until tender, about 12–15 minutes. Cool.
2. In a food-processor, blend tomato and onion to a purée. Stir in all other ingredients.
3. Cook spaghetti in boiling water on HIGH for 8–10 minutes, then strain away water. Mix tomato purée through spaghetti.
4. Fill clean recycled food jars with spaghetti mixture, cover with a metal lid.
5. Preserve and vacuum seal as per chart below.

JAR SIZE	OVEN SETTING	COOKING TIME
8 ounces	medium high	2 minutes
16 ounces	medium high	3 minutes
28 ounces	medium high	4 minutes

Note: Cooking times are for 1 jar. Add 2 minutes for every additional jar.

Check the power of your microwave and adjust the setting if necessary (see page 9).

Sweet and Sour Salsa

INGREDIENTS

½ cup diced bell pepper

1 cup gherkins, diced

2 cups sugar

1 tablespoon cornflour

2 cups crushed pineapple

2 mangoes

½ cup brown vinegar

METHOD

1. Remove skins and stones from mangoes, cut up fruit into small pieces, cut bell pepper in half and discard seeds and any pith, drain pineapple. Mix all fruits together and allow to stand for 1 hour.

2. Place sugar and one tablespoon of water into a heat-resistant microwave-proof bowl. Heat on HIGH to brown sugar (caramelize) for about 1–2 minutes.

   Note: As soon as sugar starts to brown remove from microwave. Do not stir, as this will cause sugar to crystallize.

3. Strain away excess juices from fruit. Add all ingredients to sugar (except cornflour).

4. Cook uncovered on HIGH to boiling point for 4–5 minutes, stir to dissolve sugar.

5. Blend cornflour with a little water, stir into hot salsa. Return to microwave and cook on HIGH to boiling point for 1–2 minutes or until mixture has cleared.

6. Fill clean recycled jars with hot salsa. Fit with metal lid. Cool and store.

Sweet and Sour Sauce

INGREDIENTS

3 ozs sugar

½ cup vinegar

½ cup diced gherkins

¾ cup water

1 cup pineapple pieces

METHOD

1. Place sugar and one tablespoon of water into a heat-resistant microwave-proof bowl.
2. Heat on HIGH to brown sugar (caramelize), about 1–2 minutes.
   Note: As soon as the sugar starts to brown remove from oven. Do not stir as this will cause the sugar to crystallize.
3. Add all other ingredients. Cook on HIGH for 3–4 minutes, stir to dissolve sugar.
4. To thicken sauce:
   Blend 2 tablespoons cornflour in ¼ cup water. Stir into hot sauce. Heat on HIGH to boiling point or until sauce has thickened.
5. Fill clean recycled jars with sauce, fit with a metal lid.
6. Vacuum seal according to chart below.

JAR SIZE	OVEN SETTING	COOKING TIME
8 ounces	medium high	2 minutes
28 ounces	medium high	3 minutes
28 ounces	medium high	4 minutes

Note: Cooking times are for 1 jar. Add 1 minute for every additional jar.

Check the power of your microwave and adjust the setting if necessary (see page 9).

Sweet and Spicy Strawberry Sauce

INGREDIENTS

1 lb strawberries

1 oz fresh ginger

½ teaspoon cinnamon

2 oz sugar

METHOD

1. Hull and wash strawberries. Scrape skin from ginger and grate finely.
2. Place half the strawberries and all other ingredients in a microwave-proof bowl. Cook on HIGH to boiling point for about 3–4 minutes. Stir to dissolve sugar fully.
3. Cut remaining strawberries into large pieces, stir into hot, cooked sauce. Cool.
4. Fill clean recycled jars, cover with a metal lid that has a built-in sealing ring.
5. Vacuum seal according to chart below.

JAR SIZE	OVEN SETTING	COOKING TIME
8 ounces	medium high	3 minutes
28 ounces	medium high	4 minutes
28 ounces	medium high	5 minutes

Note: Cooking times are for 1 jar. Add 2 minutes for every additional jar.

Check the power of your microwave and adjust the setting if necessary (see page 9).

Tartar Sauce

INGREDIENTS

1 cup mayonnaise
1 tablespoon white vinegar
1 tablespoon chopped gherkins
1 teaspoon mustard powder
pinch mixed herbs

METHOD

1. Stir all ingredients together in a microwave-proof bowl. Heat on MEDIUM HIGH for 1 minute. Do not allow sauce to boil.
2. Place in clean jars, seal with a lid and refrigerate. Sauce will keep 1–2 months. Serve with fish.

Tomato Sauce

INGREDIENTS

5 lbs ripe tomatoes

1 lb brown onions

¾ lb sugar

1 oz salt

1 cup spiced vinegar (see page 99)

METHOD

1. Cut tomatoes and onions up roughly. Place into a large (approximately one gallon) microwave-proof bowl. Cover with lid, cook on HIGH until tender, about 25–30 minutes. Cool.
2. Pour away some of the excess liquid. Purée tomatoes and onions in a food-processor or blender. Pour through a strainer to remove seeds and skins and return to bowl. Stir in all other ingredients.
3. Heat on HIGH uncovered to boiling point, stir to dissolve sugar. Continue boiling until sauce has thickened, about 25–35 minutes. Stir 2–3 times during this cooking time.
4. Allow to cool for 5 or 10 minutes. Fill clean sauce bottles, seal, and store.

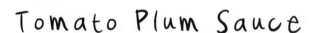

Tomato Plum Sauce

INGREDIENTS

2 lbs ripe tomatoes

2 lbs ripe plums

1 lb sugar

1½ cups vinegar

1 teaspoon salt

1 teaspoon mixed spice

½ teaspoon cayenne pepper

1 oz crushed or bruised ginger
   (**or** 1 teaspoon ground ginger)

METHOD

1. Roughly cut up all fruit and place in a microwave-proof bowl with all other ingredients.
2. Cook on HIGH for approximately 10–12 minutes.
3. Stir to dissolve sugar, then boil on HIGH for 30–40 minutes, or until sauce has thickened.
4. Allow to cool slightly and remove plum stones.
5. Purée in a food-processor or blender to a smooth sauce consistency.
6. Fill clean, warm, sterilized bottle, seal with lid.

9

Home-Dried Fruit

Dried fruit has the same nutritional value and fiber content as fresh fruit, but in a concentrated form. The microwave drying process is simple and quick, and particularly appeals to people who are sensitive or allergic to the chemicals used in most commercial drying methods. Fruit dried in your microwave is ready for use the same day or may be stored for later.

The Purpose of Drying Food

The drying process removes excess moisture from food. This inhibits the growth of molds and enzymes that would normally cause deterioration over a period of time, and thus enables the food to be stored.

In the past, food was dried in the sun or in a low-temperature oven, taking many hours or even days. The slowness of the process put a lot of people off. But now, with the wonderful invention of the microwave oven, food can be oven-dried in a very short time, making the process more appealing to a greater number of people.

The times given in this book are for a 650-watt microwave oven. However, because of variations in the wattage, always use the lowest setting possible.

Suitable Fruits

The most popular and most suitable fruits for microwave drying are apricots, bananas, apples, figs, kiwifruit, blue plums, and small grapes. Fruit used should be of first-grade quality, ripe, and free from blemishes.

Preventing Discoloration

To prevent discoloration during the drying process, all peeled fruit (such as apples and bananas) should first be washed and soaked in lemon water – a solution of 2 cups water and the juice of 1 lemon (about 3 tablespoons), or ½ teaspoon sodium metabisulfite to one cup water for 4–5 minutes. Rinse in fresh cold water before patting dry with a clean cloth.

Note: Sodium metabisulfite is available in most supermarkets labeled as sterilizing powder. Alternatively you can soak fruit in brine (a solution of 2 oz salt in 6 cups water) for 15–20 minutes. Then rinse in cold water and pat dry.

Testing the Fruit

On removal from the oven, the fruit should be dry to the touch, pliable and rubbery in texture, and, if pressed between two fingers, should recover its original bulk when released. If the right results are not achieved, return the fruit to the microwave for further drying for about 5–10 minutes on DEFROST (or the lowest possible setting). Then re-test.

Standing and Storing Dried Fruit

Once removed from the oven the fruit should be allowed to dry on a cake rack for a further 12–24 hours before being stored.

Dried fruit does not last forever. However, providing it is properly dried and stored, it will retain its optimum flavor and color for

3–5 months and may last up to 6 months. Store dried fruit in paper-lined boxes or in plastic storage bags tied at the top and punctured with one or two tiny holes. The containers should not be airtight, as the fruit will sweat. Place in a cool, dry, well-ventilated place. If mold forms, this means the fruit has not been dried properly and should be discarded.

DOs and DON'Ts

The following is a checklist of the main DOs and DON'Ts of microwave fruit drying:

- If possible choose fruits in season for best results.
- Always wash fruit thoroughly before beginning.
- Prevent discoloration by bleaching fruit in lemon water or brine before drying.
- Inspect the fruit towards the end of the drying time and remove any pieces that are ready before others.
- Dry the fruit longer than the specified time if necessary but don't over dry it.
- DON'T use fruit that is damaged or bruised or markedly under-ripe. It will lose shape and dry unevenly. Drying won't improve the food. It simply enables it to last longer.
- DON'T leave excess water on the carousel or the washed fruit – always dry with a clean cloth before beginning.
- DON'T use paper toweling on the carousel. Brown or white kitchen paper or butcher's paper is ideal.
- DON'T stack or cram fruit whilst drying – always spread in a single layer, not touching, to avoid burning and to produce more even results and fewer variations in drying time.
- DON'T slice fruit too thickly as the drying times given are for suggested sizes, and thicker or bigger pieces will not dry successfully in the given times.

Dried Apples

1. Peel and core 2 medium-sized apples. Cut into ¼ inch thick slices (about 10).
2. Soak in lemon water to prevent discoloration (see page 178).
3. Drain and pat dry.
4. Cut a circle of brown or white kitchen paper to fit the carousel.
5. Arrange apple slices in a single layer on the paper, making sure they don't touch each other.
6. Set microwave on DEFROST (or the lowest possible setting) and dry for 35–45 minutes or until dry and rubbery to touch.
7. Stand and store according to directions on page 178.

Dried Apricots

1. Choose 16–18 firm, ripe, unblemished apricots. Wash.
2. Cut in halves and remove stones.
3. Soak in lemon water to prevent discoloration (see page 178).
4. Drain and pat dry.
5. Place directly onto carousel in a single layer with cut side facing down, making sure they don't touch each other.
6. Set microwave on DEFROST (or the lowest possible setting) and dry for 50–60 minutes or until they have shriveled to about half their size and are dry and rubbery to touch.
7. Stand and store according to directions on page 178.

Dried Bananas

1. Peel 2 firm, ripe bananas under running water to help prevent discoloration. Remove any blemishes.
2. Slice into ¼ inch thick circles (about 30–40 slices).
3. Soak in lemon water to prevent discoloration (see page 178).
4. Drain and pat dry.
5. Cut a circle of brown or white kitchen paper to fit the carousel.
6. Arrange slices in a single layer on the paper, making sure they don't touch each other.
7. Set microwave on DEFROST (or the lowest possible setting) and dry for 35–45 minutes or until dry and rubbery to touch.
8. Stand and store according to directions on page 178.

Dried Grapes

1. Choose 50–60 fresh, unblemished grapes.
2. Remove stalks, wash and pat dry.
3. Cut a circle of brown or white kitchen paper to fit the carousel.
4. Spread grapes evenly in a single layer on the paper, making sure they don't touch each other.
5. Set microwave on DEFROST (or the lowest possible setting) and dry for 50–60 minutes, moving grapes around on the paper 2–3 times while drying. When ready the grapes will be about half their original size and sticky to touch.
6. Stand and store according to directions on page 178.

Dried Kiwifruit

1. Choose 4 ripe and unblemished kiwifruit and remove skins.
2. Slice into ¼ inch thick circles (about 20 slices).
3. Cut a circle of brown or white kitchen paper to fit the carousel.
4. Arrange slices in a single layer on the paper making sure they don't touch each other.
5. Set microwave on DEFROST (or the lowest possible setting) and dry for 20–30 minutes or until dry and rubbery to touch.
6. Stand and store according to directions on page 178.

Dried Mangoes

1. Choose 2 or 3 medium-sized firm and ripe mangoes.
2. Remove skin by scoring vertically at intervals and peeling down from stem. The skin will come away easily if the fruit is ripe.
3. Cut into ½ inch wedges by cutting with a knife down onto the seed and easing each segment away.
4. Cut a circle of brown or white kitchen paper to fit the carousel.
5. Arrange wedges in a single layer on the paper making sure they don't touch each other.
6. Set microwave on DEFROST (or the lowest possible setting) and dry for 40–50 minutes or until wedges have shriveled to three-quarters of their original size and are slightly sticky to touch.
7. Stand and store according to directions on page 178.

Dried Honey Mango (Variation)

1. For every mango allow 2 teaspoons honey.
2. Heat honey in a microwave-proof bowl for 30 seconds.
3. Pour over mango wedges prepared by following Steps 2–3 of *Dried Mangoes* recipe. Toss lightly to coat mangoes with honey.
4. Dry as in Steps 4–7 of *Dried Mangoes* recipe.

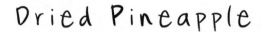

Dried Pineapple

1. Choose a ripe pineapple. To do this turn the pineapple upside-down and smell the base where the fruit was joined to the bush. If there is no smell it isn't ripe and if it smells moldy, it is overripe. When it's just right it will have a fresh fruity aroma.
2. Peel, eye, and core pineapple.
3. Cut into ¼ inch slices (about 18–24), halves or pieces.
4. Cut a circle of brown or white kitchen paper to fit the carousel.
5. Arrange pieces in a single layer on the paper, making sure they don't touch each other.
6. Set microwave on DEFROST (or the lowest possible setting) and dry for 45–60 minutes or until dry to touch and rubbery.
7. Stand and store according to directions on page 178.

Dried Plums (Prunes)

This method is for blue plums. If you use other varieties the drying time will vary slightly depending on size.

1. Choose 15–20 firm, ripe, unblemished plums.
2. If large, cut in halves and remove stones. If left whole, cut away stem or prick all over with a sterile darning needle to prevent skins from splitting.
3. Place directly onto carousel in a single layer with cut side facing down (or spread whole plums evenly), making sure they don't touch each other.
4. Set microwave on DEFROST (or the lowest possible setting) and dry for 35–45 minutes or until fruit has reduced in size and is dry to touch.
5. Stand and store according to directions on page 178.

Dried Tomatoes

1. Choose firm, ripe tomatoes, e.g. mama mia, roma, cherry, or sweet bite (marble-sized).
2. Cut small tomatoes into halves (lengthwise if egg-shaped and small) or large tomatoes into ½ inch slices.
3. Arrange directly on carousel in a single layer, cut side up, making sure they don't touch each other.
4. Set microwave on DEFROST (or the lowest possible setting) and dry for approximately 25–45 minutes (the time varies according to ripeness and size) or until shriveled and dry to touch.

10

Glacé and Crystallized Fruit

Glacé and crystallized fruit can be bought ready prepared, but tends to be rather expensive. The microwave method of glazing and crystallizing is quick and effective, causing very little damage to color, flavor, texture, and nutritional content. The finished product makes an attractive decoration for desserts or a special treat with after-dinner coffee or liqueurs. A box of glacé or crystallized fruits makes a luxurious gift.

Suitable Fruits

Firm fruits such as apricots, grapes, peaches, plums, and pineapple give the best results. Ginger and the peel or whole-fruit slices of citrus fruit are very successful. The fruit should be of top quality, ripe but firm, and without blemishes. Soft fruits such as berries are not suitable as they tend to break up and go mushy during the cooking process.

Preparing the Fruit

Fruit to be glazed or crystallized whole should be pricked with a large sterilized darning needle to allow the syrup to penetrate the skin. Larger fruits should be peeled and halved or quartered.

Storing the Fruit

Glacé or crystallized fruit should not be stored in airtight containers. For best results, store in a small cardboard box lined with waxed paper and covered with a lid. Layers of fruit can thus be separated by sheets of waxed paper to prevent sticking. If glass jars are used, do not cover with lids as the fruit will go moldy due to lack of ventilation. Place in a cool, dry, airy place, where it will keep for 6–12 months.

Glazing Syrup

When making syrup, observe the following points for best results:

- If a sugar thermometer is used to confirm cooking times the correct temperature is easily ascertained. However, if you do not have one of these, the next best method is to test for "pulling consistency". After 1 or 2 minutes of boiling, drop a tablespoon of syrup into a cup of cold water. When the cooled syrup is transparent and can be stretched a little without breaking, the desired temperature has been achieved.
- You must ensure that the syrup does not crystallize while being boiled. To do this, do not stir when you first add water to the sugar. At the next stage, ensure that every single grain of sugar is dissolved or removed as directed. Just one remaining grain of sugar will cause crystallization and render your syrup useless.
- Once the syrup has reached its correct temperature of consistency try not to disturb unnecessarily when dunking fruit.
- It is not advisable to glaze different varieties of fruit in the same syrup as the individual flavor can be lost.

Glazing Syrup

INGREDIENTS
¼ cup water or cooking liquid from fruit
1 cup sugar
½ teaspoon cream of tartar

METHOD
1. Place sugar in a microwave-proof bowl, add water carefully so as not to disturb sugar. Do NOT stir.
2. Cover and heat on HIGH for 1–2 minutes, until just below boiling point.
3. Now stir to fully dissolve sugar. Use a damp pastry brush to brush away any grains of sugar around the sides of the bowl.
4. When satisfied that all sugar is dissolved and syrup is completely clear, stir in cream of tartar (this inhibits crystallization).
5. Return to microwave and boil on HIGH for approximately 3 minutes, or until syrup has reached 200°F on a sugar thermometer, or until syrup is of a light "pulling consistency" when tested in cold water (see page 187).

Glazing the Fruit

METHOD
1. Add the fruit to the hot syrup. Return to microwave and continue boiling until fruit is just tender but still holds it shape – approximately 1–2 minutes.
2. Remove the bowl from the microwave and allow fruit to stand in syrup until transparent (about 10–12 minutes).

3. Remove fruit and arrange on a cake cooler to drain away excess syrup.

4. Return uncovered bowl to microwave, set on HIGH and bring syrup back to boiling point (about 1–2 minutes).

5. Place each piece of fruit separately on a skewer or draining spoon and dunk into the hot syrup.

6. Allow excess syrup to drip away for a minute or so before drying in the microwave.

Drying the Glacé Fruit

METHOD

1. Cut a circle of brown or white kitchen paper to fit the carousel.

2. Arrange fruit slices in a single layer on the paper, making sure they don't touch each other.

2. Set microwave on DEFROST and dry for 15–20 minutes or until slightly sticky.

3. Allow to stand on a cake cooler for 12 hours, then store according to directions on page 187.

Note: For 500–550-watt microwave ovens, about 10 minutes extra drying time will be necessary. On the other hand, 700–750 watt ovens will take about 10 minutes less time to dry the fruit.

Crystallizing the Fruit

Glacé fruit is delicious, but some people prefer crystallized fruit. To make this, you simply take your glacé fruit and dunk it in boiling water. Then you toss it in granulated sugar until well-coated.

Glacé Apricots

INGREDIENTS
10–12 apricots
Glazing Syrup (see page 188)

METHOD
1. Wash and dry apricots. If large, cut in half, if small, leave whole. Prick surface with a sterilized darning needle to allow syrup to penetrate.
2. Follow Steps 1–6 of *Glazing the Fruit* (page 188) and Steps 1–4 of *Drying the Fruit* (pages 189).

Glacé Cumquats

INGREDIENTS
8–10 cumquats
Glazing Syrup (see page 188)

METHOD
1. If cumquats are large, cut in half, if not, prepare as directed on page 186.
2. Place cumquats in syrup, set microwave on HIGH and boil 6–8 minutes.
3. Follow Steps 2–6 of *Glazing the Fruit* (page 188).
4. Dry cumquats on DEFROST for 15–20 minutes or until slightly sticky to touch.
5. Allow to stand on a cake cooler for 12 hours before storing (see page 187).

Glacé Ginger

INGREDIENTS

4 ozs fresh ginger

Glazing Syrup (see page 188)

METHOD

1. Peel or scrape outer skin from ginger. Cut into rounds ¼ inch thick.
2. Place ginger in syrup, set microwave on HIGH and boil for 6–8 minutes or until slightly transparent.
3. Follow Steps 3–6 of *Glazing the Fruit* (page 188).
4. Dry ginger on DEFROST for 10–15 minutes or until slightly sticky to touch.
5. Allow to stand on a cake cooler for 12 hours before storing (see page 187).

Glacé Grapes

INGREDIENTS
24–30 large grapes
Glazing Syrup (see page 188)

METHOD
1. Use scissors to cut each grape from the bunch, leaving about ¼ inch of stem attached to each grape. Wash gently in cold water and pat dry.
2. Prick each grape 5–6 times with a darning needle to prevent skins bursting during cooking and to allow syrup to penetrate.
3. Follow Steps 1–6 of *Glazing the Fruit* (page 188) and Steps 1–4 of *Drying the Fruit* (page 189).

Glacé Kiwifruit

INGREDIENTS
4–5 kiwifruit
Glazing Syrup (see page 188)

METHOD
1. Peel and slice each kiwifruit into ½ inch slices.
2. Follow Steps 1–6 of *Glazing the Fruit* (page 188) and Steps 1–4 of *Drying the Fruit* (page 189).

Glacé Orange and Lemon Peel

INGREDIENTS

2 oranges

2 lemons

2 cups water for cooking peel

Glazing Syrup (see page 188)

Soaking Solution

2 cups water for soaking peel

1 teaspoon baking soda dissolved in 2 cups water

METHOD

1. Remove zest from fruit with a vegetable peeler (do not peel into pith).
2. Cut peel into strips of about ½ inch x ½ inch.
3. To enhance color soak peel for 20 minutes in soaking solution.
4. Drain and wash peel.
5. Place with water in a microwave-proof bowl and boil on high for 8–10 minutes.
6. Stand to cool, about 20 minutes. Strain away water.
7. Place peel in syrup, set microwave on HIGH and boil for 5–6 minutes or until slightly transparent.
8. Follow Steps 2–6 of *Glazing the Fruit* (page 188).
9. Dry peel on DEFROST for 10–12 minutes or until slightly sticky.
10. Allow to stand on a cake cooler for 12 hours before storing (see page 187).

Glacé Peaches

INGREDIENTS
10–12 medium-sized yellow-fleshed peaches
Glazing Syrup (see page 188)

METHOD
1. Wash, dry, and halve peaches. If fruit is very large, use only 6–8 and cut into quarters. Remove stones.
2. Follow Steps 1–6 of *Glazing the Fruit* (page 188) and Steps 1–4 of *Drying the Fruit* (page 189).

Glacé Pineapple

INGREDIENTS
1 medium-sized pineapple
Glazing Syrup (see page 188)

METHOD
1. Remove all skin and eyes from pineapple.
2. Cut in ¼ inch thick circles. Remove core. Use whole, halved or quartered.
3. Follow Steps 1–6 of *Glazing the Fruit* (page 188) and Steps 1–4 of *Drying the Fruit* (page 189).

Glacé Plums

INGREDIENTS

18–24 plums

Glazing Syrup (see page 188)

METHOD

1. Wash and dry plums. If large, cut in half; if small leave whole. Prick surface with a sterilized darning needle to allow syrup to penetrate.
2. Follow Steps 1–6 of *Glazing the Fruit* (page 188) and Steps 1–4 of *Drying the Fruit* (pages 189).

11

Fruity Liqueurs

Fruit liqueurs are made from natural fruit juices in an alcohol base. They are less expensive than the commercial equivalent and are fun to make, as well as being a source of pride as you serve them to friends with after-dinner coffee.

To prepare a fruit liqueur the fruit is first cooked in the microwave for a few minutes to extract the juices and flavor, then sugar is added to sweeten, and finally the whole is combined with a spirit-based alcohol, for example brandy or gin.

The liqueur must be allowed to infuse for up to a week before being strained and bottled. (Sterilize bottles by covering bottom with one inch of water and cooking on HIGH until boiling. Pour boiling water into and over lids and let stand for 2–3 minutes. Drain water away.) A final maturing time of at least a month is necessary before serving, to achieve full bloom and flavor.

With their vivid color and luster, attractively bottled fruit liqueurs make a most acceptable gift.

Apricot Liqueur

INGREDIENTS
1 lb fresh apricots
1 teaspoon ground allspice
1 lb sugar
3 cups dry white wine
2½ cups gin

METHOD
1. Choose well-ripened apricots and wash clean. Halve and remove stones.
2. Place fruit in a large microwave-proof bowl along with sugar, allspice, and wine.
3. Cook on HIGH until boiling (about 5–6 minutes).
4. Stir to dissolve sugar. Cool. Add gin.
5. Cover bowl with a lid or plastic wrap and leave for 5–6 days to infuse.
6. Strain liqueur through a very fine strainer or muslin, squeezing out as much liquid as possible.
7. Fill clean, sterilized wine bottles, and cork or seal.
8. Store in a cool place for at least one month before serving.

Apricots in Liqueur

These apricots are delicious served with natural yogurt or cream.

INGREDIENTS

2 lbs fresh apricots

Apricot Liqueur (see previous recipe)

METHOD

1. Choose small to medium, firm apricots and wash clean.
2. Place whole fruit in a clean, sterilized jar.
3. Pour over apricot liqueur to within half an inch of the top of the jar. Cover with lid.
4. Store in a cool place for at least one months before using.

Cherry Brandy

INGREDIENTS

1 lb cherries

4 ozs sugar

3 whole cloves

3½ cups brandy

METHOD

1. Wash cherries and remove stones.
2. Place fruit and sugar in a microwave-proof bowl and cook on HIGH for 3–4 minutes or until cherries have softened slightly.
3. Remove from oven and allow to cool. Add cloves and brandy. Cover bowl with a lid or plastic wrap.
4. Allow to mature for 10–12 weeks.
5. Strain brandy through a very fine strainer or muslin, squeezing out as much liquid as possible.
6. Fill clean, sterilized wine bottles, and cork or seal.
7. Store in a cool place for at least one month before serving.

Crystallized Fruit in Cognac

A single crystallized fruit or a combination of fruits in liqueur is delicious served with cream or ice-cream on a special occasion.

INGREDIENTS

whole pieces of crystallized fruit (see Chapter 11)

cognac

METHOD

1. Clean and sterilize suitably sized jars and lids.
2. Fill jars with crystallized fruit.
3. Pour cognac over to within ½ inch of the top of the jar. Cover with lid.
4. Store in a cool place for at least one month before using.

Peach Brandy

INGREDIENTS
1 lb yellow-fleshed peaches (clingstone or queen)
4 ozs sugar
½ teaspoon ground nutmeg
2½ cups brandy

METHOD
1. Leaving skins on, wash peaches, halve, and remove stones. Slice roughly.
2. Place fruit, sugar, and nutmeg in a microwave-proof bowl and cook on HIGH for 2–3 minutes.
3. Remove from oven and allow to cool. Add brandy. Cover bowl with a lid or plastic wrap.
4. Allow to mature for 10–14 days.
5. Strain brandy through a very fine strainer or muslin, squeezing out as much liquid as possible.
6. Fill clean, sterilized wine bottles, and cork or seal.
7. Store in a cool place for at least one month before serving.

Raspberry Gin

INGREDIENTS
¾ lb fresh or preserved raspberries

3 ozs sugar

2 cups gin

METHOD
1. If fresh, choose firm, unblemished raspberries. Hull, wash, and dry.
2. Place fruit, sugar, and gin in a glass container or bottle, stir and seal with plastic wrap or a cork.
3. Allow to mature in a cool place for at least 3 months, occasionally stirring or shaking gently.
4. Strain gin through a very fine strainer or muslin. Fill clean, sterilized wine bottle, and cork or seal.

The leftover raspberries are great as a dessert served with ice-cream.

Strawberry or Blackberry Liqueur

INGREDIENTS

1 lb sugar

6–8 whole cloves

1 cup brandy

For berry juice:

2 lbs ripe berries

1 cup water

METHOD

1. Place berries and water into a microwave-proof bowl.
1. Cook on HIGH for 5–8 minutes to extract juice.
3. Strain and measure up 4 cups of juice. (The remaining fruit can be chilled and used as a sweet.)
4. Place juice and sugar in a large microwave-proof bowl and cook on HIGH until boiling, about 5–6 minutes. Stir to dissolve sugar.
5. Add cloves and return syrup to microwave. Cook on HIGH a further 5–6 minutes.
6. Cool. Add brandy.
7. Cover bowl with a lid or plastic wrap and leave for 3 days to infuse.
8. Strain liqueur through a very fine strainer or muslin, squeezing out as much liquid as possible.
9 Fill clean, sterilized wine bottles, and cork or seal.
10. Store in a cool place for at least one month before serving.

Sultana Grapes in Berry Liqueur

INGREDIENTS
1 large bunch ripe grapes
Berry Liqueur (see page 204)

METHOD
1. Using scissors, cut each grape from the bunch leaving approximately ¼ inch of stem attached to each grape. Wash gently in cold water and pat dry.
2. Place grapes carefully in clean, sterilized jars.
3. Pour over Berry Liqueur to within ½ inch of the top of the jar. Cover with lid.
4. Store in a cool place for at least one month before using.

12

Fruity Drinks

In summer, there's nothing quite as refreshing as home-made fruit drinks. Apart from the alcoholic apple cider, they are ideal for children as well as adults.

Apple Cider (alcoholic)

INGREDIENTS

24 medium apples (jonathans or Granny Smiths)

¼ cup hops

6–8 cups water

1 cup sugar

extra water

METHOD

1. Roughly cut unpeeled/uncored apples into small pieces.
2. Place into a large microwave-proof bowl. Heat in microwave on HIGH, 10–23 minutes.
3. In another bowl, place 5 cups of water, sugar, and hops. Heat to boiling point. Stir to dissolve sugar. Pour over apples. Add extra boiling water to cover apples if not covered fully. Stand for 24 hours.
4. Strain through a fine strainer and fill clean bottles.
5. Add 1 raisin to each bottle before firmly sealing. Store for one week in a warm cupboard.
6. Chill before serving.

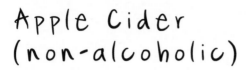

Apple Cider (non-alcoholic)

INGREDIENTS

apples (jonathans or Granny Smiths)
sugar
boiling water

METHOD

1. Roughly cut unpeeled/uncored apples into small pieces.
    Place into a large bowl or bucket.
2. Cover with boiling water. Stir
3. Allow to stand uncovered to three days. Strain through a fine
    strainer.
4. To every 5 cups of apple liquid, add 1 cup of sugar. Stir to dissolve
    sugar. Stand another three days.
5. Fill clean bottles and seal. Store in cupboard for one week.
    Chill before serving.

Ginger Beer

INGREDIENTS

1 oz ground ginger

5 pints boiling water

1½ lbs sugar

2 level teaspoons cream of tartar

1 large lemon, juice and rind

1½ teaspoons dried yeast

METHOD

1. Grate rind from lemon, squeeze out juice. Place into a large container with all other ingredients except yeast. Stir to dissolve sugar.
2. Allow to stand until just warm (blood temperature) stir in yeast.
3. Allow to stand in a warm place for 24 hours.
4. Skim off any scum and gently pour liquid into a clean container, leaving all sediment behind.
5. Fill clean bottles and seal tightly with a lid.
6. Allow ginger beer to stand for at least 3 days before using.
7. It is a good idea to store ginger beer somewhere that won't matter if a lid decides to pop off and beer spills.

Lemonade

INGREDIENTS

6–8 lemons

2 cups water

2 cups sugar

8 cups extra water

METHOD

1. Peel the rind from 4 lemons very thinly. Place sugar, 2 cups water, and lemon rind into a microwave-proof bowl. Heat to boiling point on HIGH, about 3–4 minutes. Stir to dissolve sugar. Remove and discard rind. Cool.
2. Stir in the juice of the lemons and the 8 cups of water before serving chilled.

Pomegranate Juice

INGREDIENTS

pomegranates

sugar to taste

lemon juice, (allow two tablespoons to each cup of juice)

METHOD

1. To extract juice: warm pomegranates in microwave on HIGH for from 30 seconds to 1 minute. Gently roll between hands several times.
2. Make a small hole in the base of the fruit with a knife or skewer. Set the pomegranate over a glass and allow the juice to drain. Every now and then press the fruit to extract all the juice. Add lemon juice and sugar to taste.
3. Fill clean, sterilized, recycled jars with juice. Cover with a metal lid which has a built-in sealing ring.
4. Preserve and vacuum seal as from chart below.

JAR SIZE	OVEN SETTING	COOKING TIME
8 ounces	medium high	2 minutes
16 ounces	medium high	3 minutes
28 ounces	medium high	4 minutes

Note: Cooking times are for 1 jar. Add 2 minutes for every additional jar.

Check the power of your microwave and adjust the setting if necessary (see page 9).

Raspberry Vinegar Drink

INGREDIENTS

2 lbs raspberries

2 cups malt vinegar

2 lbs sugar (approx.)

METHOD

1. Wash and dry raspberries. Place in a microwave-proof bowl and crush with a wooden spoon or fork.
2. Pour over the vinegar and set aside, covered for 5–6 days. Stir once or twice each day.
3. Strain the raspberry vinegar liquid through muslin or a fine strainer. Do not press berry pulp through.
4. To every cup of liquid, add ¾ lb of sugar. Stir together.
5. Place in the microwave and heat on HIGH to boiling point. Stir to dissolve sugar fully. Continue cooking on MEDIUM HIGH for 4–5 minutes.
6. Allow to cool. Fill clean bottles, seal with lid firmly.
7. To serve, dilute with water and ice cubes. Raspberry vinegar makes a refreshing drink, or diluted with hot water, can help a sore throat or cold.

Refreshing Fruit Punch

INGREDIENTS

3 oranges

3 lemons

1 cup mint, freshly chopped

1 cup sugar

1 cup lime juice concentrate

2 pints dry ginger ale

2 pints lemon-lime soda

2 cups water

METHOD

1. Slice unpeeled oranges and lemons. Place into large microwave-proof bowl. Add mint, cook on HIGH for 1–2 minutes. Mix in sugar and press firmly with a wooden spoon to bruise fruit and release juices.

2. Add lime juice and water, and on serving add dry ginger and lemon-lime soda. Serve cold with ice cubes.

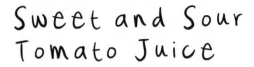

Sweet and Sour Tomato Juice

INGREDIENTS

4 lbs ripe tomatoes

2½ cups sugar

1 cup vinegar

6 whole cloves

1 inch cinnamon stick

METHOD

1. Scald tomatoes in boiling water for 1–2 minutes and remove skins then slice finely.
2. Put tomatoes and vinegar in a large microwave-proof bowl, cook on HIGH to boiling point. Continue boiling on HIGH a further 5–8 minutes. Cool.
3. Strain juice from tomatoes. Return to bowl. Stir in sugar and spices.
4. Strain into a jug for easy pouring. Fill clean jars and cover with a metal lid that is fitted with a built-in sealing ring.
5. Vacuum seal as from chart below.

JAR SIZE	OVEN SETTING	COOKING TIME
8 ounces	medium high	2 minutes
16 ounces	medium high	3 minutes
28 ounces	medium high	4 minutes

Note: Cooking times are for 1 jar. Add 2 minutes for every additional jar.

Check the power of your microwave and adjust the setting if necessary (see page 9).

Tangy Fruit Drink

INGREDIENTS

4 lbs fruit, overripe of your choice

2 pints water

Sugar to taste

METHOD

1. Remove stones from fruit if necessary.
2. Cut fruit into small chunks, add sugar to taste.
3. Place in a microwave-proof bowl and heat to boiling point on HIGH for about 3–4 minutes. Stir to dissolve sugar. Allow to cool.
4. Cover with water, mix well. Leave to ferment for 3–4 days, stirring twice each day.
5. Strain through muslin or a fine strainer into a clean bowl or jar. Do not cover so that it is exposed to the air. (The more air the quicker it turns to vinegar).
6. To serve, dilute fruit drink with ice cubes.

13

Fruit Sorbets

Sorbet is a frozen mixture made from sweetened fruit purée, fruit juices or milk, egg whites, and sometimes gelatin, depending on the acidity of the fruit. Traditionally, sorbet was served between courses at formal dinners, to clean the palate. These days, it is more commonly served at informal dinners as part of a refreshing dessert, along with cold fruit – especially appealing in warm weather.

It is important to taste the sorbet before freezing, so that more sugar can be added if necessary. Sorbet is served in a glass or a sweets dish as it is too soft to mold.

Banana Sorbet

INGREDIENTS

2 cups mashed banana

¼ cup lemon juice

½ cup sugar

1 egg white

2 cups milk

METHOD

1. Purée banana by blending or passing through a coarse sieve. Add lemon juice and sugar.
2. Beat egg white until stiff, fold into banana, and slowly stir in milk.
3. Freeze in freezer trays for 1 hour. Remove from trays and beat until smooth. Return mixture to trays and refreeze until just firm.

Cherry Sorbet

INGREDIENTS

2½ cups fresh cherries

¾ cups sugar

¼ teaspoon almond extract

3 cups milk

METHOD

1. Wash and pit cherries. Blend to a pulp before measuring. Make up 2½ cups of fruit and juice together.
2. Add sugar to pulp, place in a microwave-proof bowl, cover and heat on HIGH until boiling (about 2–3 minutes).
3. Remove and stir to dissolve sugar.
4. Add almond extract and milk.
5. Freeze in freezer trays for 1 hour before serving.

Mango Sorbet

INGREDIENTS
2 large, ripe mangoes
  (or 1 cup mango purée)
½ cup sugar
1½ cups water
⅓ cup lemon juice
2 egg whites

METHOD
1. Skin mangoes and remove flesh from seed. Purée flesh by blending until smooth.
2. Combine sugar and water in microwave-proof bowl. Heat on HIGH until boiling for about 2–3 minutes.
3. Remove and stir to dissolve sugar.
4. Return syrup to oven and boil on HIGH for a further 5–6 minutes. Cool.
5. Stir in mango purée and lemon juice.
6. Freeze in freezer trays until just firm, for approximately 1 hour. Remove from trays and beat until smooth.
7. Beat egg white until stiff and fluffy, and fold into mango mixture until smooth.
8. Return mixture to trays and refreeze.

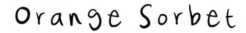

Orange Sorbet

INGREDIENTS

2 cups fresh orange juice

1½ cups sugar

1 cup water

3 tablespoons lemon juice

2 egg whites

METHOD

1. Combine sugar and water in microwave-proof bowl. Heat on HIGH for 2 minutes.
2. Remove and stir to dissolve sugar. Cool.
3. Beat egg whites until stiff and gradually beat in cooled syrup, lemon, and orange juice.
4. Pour into freezer trays and freeze for about 1 hour, or until partially frozen.
5. Remove from trays and spoon into a bowl. Beat until smooth but not fully melted.
6. Return mixture to trays and refreeze.

Grapefruit or a combination of grapefruit and orange juice can be used in place of orange and lemon juices.

Pineapple Sorbet

INGREDIENTS

2 cups crushed pineapple

1 cup sugar

2 cups water or pineapple juice

2 cups cream

METHOD

1. Place sugar and water in a microwave-proof bowl. Cover and heat on HIGH until boiling. Boil for 2 minutes.
2. Remove and cool.
3. Add all other ingredients and mix together.
4. Freeze in freezer trays for 1 hour.
5. Remove from trays and beat until smooth.
6. Return mixture to trays and refreeze.

Rhubarb and Strawberry Sorbet

INGREDIENTS

2½ cups strawberries

2 cups cooked rhubarb

2 tablespoons lemon juice

1½ cups sugar

¾ cup cream

METHOD

1. Wash berries, hull, and mash. Purée rhubarb and berries by blending or pressing through a coarse sieve.
2. Stir in all other ingredients.
3. Freeze in freezer trays until just firm (about 1 hour).
4. Just before serving, scrape up thin layers of the mixture with a large spoon. Place in a bowl and stir until smooth. Serve immediately.

Index